THE REVIVALS OF THE BIBLE

THE REVIVALS

OF THE

BIBLE

REV. ERNEST BAKER

First Printed 1906
This edition 1988

© Ambassador Productions Ltd. 1988

ISBN 0 907927 30 0

Printed and Published by:
Ambassador Productions Ltd.
Providence House
Belfast BT5 6JR

FOREWORD

Today there is a renewed interest in the subject of revival. The re-print of this book 'The Revivals of the Bible' by Rev. Ernest Baker, I believe will help Ministers and Christian leaders to have a clear understanding of the Biblical background and characteristics of genuine revival. Many Christians today, still confuse revival with evangelism, but evangelism is what the Church does for God, whereas revival or spiritual awakening is what God does for the Church.

This series of messages on the Revivals of the Bible, remind us that scriptural revival is a sovereign work of God on behalf of His Church. It was Matthew Henry who said, 'When God intends great mercy for His people, He first of all sets them a-praying'.

My prayer is that the readers of this book will be stirred to cry to God like the Psalmist, 'Wilt thou not revive us again, that thy people may rejoice in thee?' (Psalm 85 : 6).

Rev Stanley Barnes
Hillsborough
Co. Down

October 1988

CONTENTS.

I.

In Egypt.

" And Moses and Aaron went and gathered together all the elders of the children of Israel; and Aaron spake all the words which the Lord had spoken unto Moses, and did the signs in the sight of the people. And the people believed; and when they heard that the Lord had visited the children of Israel, and that He had seen their affliction, then they bowed their heads and worshipped.—EXODUS iv. 29—31.

A STUDY of the revivals of the Bible will enable us to understand what kind of revival God is ready to give. It will also serve as a guide for intelligent prayer and effort in this direction. I intend to speak of revival in the popular sense, dealing with the cases where multitudes turned to the Lord. The first of this character is reported as taking place in the northern part of Africa.

The children of Israel were brought out of Egypt by means of miracle and revival. The plagues were God's arguments with Pharoah. Against his will he was compelled to let the people go. But the Israelites were not forced out. They were consenting parties to the exodus. Before they left the country they had been brought to faith in and obedience to God. In the list of the heroes of faith recorded in the eleventh chapter of the Epistle to the Hebrews, we find the Israelites included. "By faith they passed through the Red Sea as by dry land." The story of this revival centres our thoughts around three characters—the Reviver, the Revived, and the Revivalists.

I.—THE REVIVER.

This revival was of God. He heard their cry. This was not necessarily directed to Him. It was the cry of distress. Their oppressed condition appealed to Him. He was moved with compassion. He said : "I have surely seen the affliction of My people which are in Egypt, and have heard their cry by reason of their taskmasters ; for I know their sorrows ; and I am come down to deliver them out of the hand of the Egyptians." Mingled with the compassion was indignation with their oppressors. "I have seen," He said, "the oppression wherewith the Egyptians oppress them." He could not look on, unmoved, at the injustice that was being dealt out to them. He also remembered His covenant which He had made with Abraham, Isaac, and Jacob, to give the land of Canaan to their seed. And because His word awaited fulfilment He said He would bring the children of Israel out of Egypt. Being moved with compassion for their sorrows, with indignation at their wrongs, and with a desire to fulfil His word, He called Moses to be their deliverer. Moses was not willing to undertake the work, and God had a long controversy with him concerning the matter. It was God who called Moses, persuaded him, commissioned him, and strengthened him for the task. Note therefore :

1. *God can Revive.* A revival is a Divine thing. It is a putting forth of Divine strength. It is God visiting the people. A revival cannot be organised any more than the spring. " Thou renewest the face of the ground." Men watch the coming of spring and avail themselves of it. They plough the ground and sow the seed, but it is God who gives the rain and the sunshine, and who makes the juices of the trees and of the grasses to flow. In like manner the renewing of spiritual life is God's work.

2. *God wants to Revive.* The revival in Egypt was not only a manifestation of God's power, but an act of Divine grace. His heart was in the work. He visited the people because He was moved with compassion. He is not indifferent to the world's needs. Over and over again, when spiritual life has seemed to be on the point of extinction, God has stepped in and has saved both it and the people. The history of revivals is the story of God stepping in to save faith and morals from death. Each revival

in the history of Israel came when religion was low. It means ruin for the people when faith is eclipsed ; and God will not allow the world to be utterly lost. The revivals of Christianity have occurred when the funeral of the faith has seemed nigh. When the Christian church was corrupt, impure, tyrannical, and generally in a scandalous condition, the Reformation came, and the people were led back to a purifying and helpful faith. When religion in England in the eighteenth century was cold and formal, when literature was atheistic, when the working people were living like brutes, the great evangelical revival, under Wesley and Whitefield, took place. And now—when men are telling us that the church has lost its hold of the masses, when a church census reveals that the most Christian of our cities has only one in six of its people attending worship, when the prevailing temper of the people is one of utter indifference to God, and complete absorption in the race for wealth or the pursuit of pleasure—God has stepped in and given us an evidence of His power and of His living interest in men's welfare by the revival in Wales. In South Africa the spirit of the times is manifest in every town and village. Indifference to God characterizes the overwhelming majority of our people. The breath of God's Spirit is needed to save faith and character, and to heal the land. And the visitation that is required, God is waiting to give.

3. *God will Revive.* His Word abides. Over 400 years earlier His promise to Abraham had been given. The centuries had not made His promise obsolete. Many men consider an old promise obsolete though unfulfilled. But it is not so with God. The promises of revival still hold good. God said to Solomon : "If My people, which are called by My name, shall humble themselves, and pray, and seek My face, and turn from their wicked ways; then will I hear from heaven, and will forgive their sin, and will heal their land." The promise of that word abides ; and wherever the conditions of it are fulfilled the promise will be realized. Again, in the New Testament : "Repent, and turn again, that your sins may be blotted out, that so there may come seasons of refreshing from the presence of the Lord." God is always willing to fulfil His Word ; and if we listen and look to Him we may expect revival in our land.

II.—THE REVIVED.

1. *They were a backslidden people.* They were the children of Abraham, Isaac, and Jacob, and they had been brought up in the faith. When they entered Egypt they were a chastened, God-fearing company, but in the course of years they had sunk to the level of the life around them. Joshua tells us that the people served other gods in Egypt. The worship of the golden calf in the wilderness was a

return to the religion to which they had become accustomed.

A revival in the southern portion of the same continent over 3,000 years later will mean a return of backslidden people to the Lord. History has repeated itself. In Africa men have forgotten their fathers' God, and succumbed to the influences of the life around them. The people outside of our churches, who make a holiday of a holy day, are not ignorant of God. They knew a church life at home ; they came to us from godly homes ; many of them have been in the Sunday schools of the older countries. Others, occasionally in our churches, were once more regular in their attendance upon the means of grace, and active in Christian service. A revival will mean a call to these to return to the faith of their fathers and to their first love. God is waiting to welcome such. He is ready to bless. Each backslider who returns will help to bring a blessing. Each returning one will encourage others.

2. *They were a poor and an oppressed people.* They were enslaved. Their days were spent under the lash. They knew no day of rest. It was toil from early morn to late at night, from youth to old age. Their social conditions were radically wrong. But Moses did not wait for an improvement in their earthly lot before preaching to them the word of the Lord. They attained to faith before a commercial or social revival came. The spiritual was

first, the temporal came as a result. There are many social conditions around us that need altering, and injustices that require attention. But legislation moves slowly. In the meantime we need not wait for better temporal circumstances before seeking for spiritual improvement. A revival of spiritual life is the quickest way to improve social conditions. A revived spititual life means a quickened conscience all round. A new man means a new home, new homes mean new streets, new streets mean a new city. And an interest in the public welfare comes to the new man. A quickened conscience will put into operation good laws which are now practically a dead letter because of the lack of a healthy public opinion to make them effective ; and it will also be productive of better legislation to remedy other evils still awaiting improved laws.

And just as we do not need to wait for social reform before having a revival of spiritual life, so we do not need to wait for commercial revival before receiving an increase of spiritual blessing. Commercial depression and poverty must necessarily curtail schemes of church extension, and put a stop to building efforts ; but no money is wanted to bring a revival. The spiritual life can be increased without the outlay of an additional penny. God can, and will, revive a poor and a distressed people if they only look to Him.

III.—THE REVIVALISTS.

1. *Moses and Aaron gathered the people.* The text says that Moses and Aaron gathered the elders ; but as the narrative speaks of the presence of the people, we conclude that the people were brought together through the elders. The assembling of the people is our united work. There are people to be gathered, and they need to be gathered in order to hear the Word of the Lord. If the services at God's house are helpful to us we should talk about them. We should make it known that a good thing is on, and endeavour to get others to the place where our spiritual life receives help.

2. *They preached the Word.* All revivals have been accompanied with preaching. God's Spirit works through the Word. The revival in Wales is no exception ; though temporarily, in many cases, the sermon was pushed on one side. But this was because all the Lord's people became prophets. The rank and file testified. Preaching, however, is more highly regarded in Wales now than ever. The new converts want instruction. "It pleased God by the foolishness of preaching to save them that believe." Let us know the words which the Lord hath spoken, and tell them out to others.

3. *They did the signs.* What are the signs which God empowers us to give in order to win men to the faith ? "By this shall all men know that ye are My disciples, if ye have love one to

another." "The nations shall know that I am the Lord, when I shall be sanctified in you before their eyes." If quarrels are made up ; if fault-finding and backbiting are discontinued ; if we cease to be self-centred and learn to take a warm-hearted interest in others ; if we are honest and pay our debts ; and if we become contented, patient, and forgiving, signs will be given which will help men to believe.

II.

In the Times of the Judges.

"And the children of Israel cried unto the Lord."—
Judges x. 10.

THERE are five seasons of Revival recorded in
the book of Judges. The phrase, "the
children of Israel cried unto the Lord," occurs in
connection with each of these occasions. Each
time the prayer comes after a long period of oppression. The same kind of circumstances accompany
it. They forsake the Lord and serve the gods of
other nations. Then they come into bondage to
those nations whose gods they serve. After years of
oppression they repent and cry to God. Each time
He hears them, and sends them a saviour and
deliverer.

This is the story in brief : They served the
King of Mesopotamia eight years, "and when the
children of Israel cried unto the Lord, the Lord
raised up a saviour . . . Othniel." They were
in bondage to Moab eighteen years, and "when the
children of Israel cried unto the Lord, the Lord
raised them up a saviour . . . Ehud." They

were in bondage to Jabin, King of Canaan, twenty years, "and the children of Israel cried unto the Lord"; and Deborah and Barak were given in response to that cry. "And Israel was brought very low because of Midian (after seven years), and the children of Israel cried unto the Lord," and the Lord sent a prophet . . . and Gideon. Then they were in bondage to the Philistines and to the children of Ammon for eighteen years, "and the children of Israel cried unto the Lord," and His answer was Jephthah.

It is the same story each time. The only alteration is in the name of the people to whom they were in bondage, the name of the deliverer sent in answer to their prayer, and the number of years in which they were held in bondage. In all the cases, except the last, we simply have the record "the children of Israel cried unto the Lord." What they said we do not know. In the last case, however, we have their prayer recorded; and I have no doubt that it is a fair specimen of the prayers of former occasions. They said: "We have sinned against Thee, both because we have forsaken our God, and also served Baalim."

The revivals in the times of the Judges show that prayer occupies a principal part in the return of any people to the Lord. And the word "cry" is suggestive of the type of prayer that issues in blessing. It is the word most frequently used in the Old

Testament to describe prayer.   It speaks of distress.
We cry out when we are in trouble.   When Peter
was sinking in the water he cried, " Lord, save me."
The word cry tells of a distress that is felt.   These
people had been in uncomfortable circumstances for
years, but the full meaning of their lot had not
come home to them, and distressed their spirits,
until now.   But now they feel the shame and
disgrace of their condition.   The word suggests a
need that is urgent.   Peter could not wait for help
when he cried.   He wanted assistance at once.
These people said : " Only deliver us, we pray Thee,
this day."   The word also speaks of a feeling of
helplessness.   They require some power from outside to come to their relief.   They are in bondage.
They cannot deliver themselves.   They want a leader,
a saviour.

Men are in bondage to sin, and they are uncon-
cerned.   They are content with their bonds.   They
do not feel the shame and the disgrace of their
position.   And, whilst in that condition, there is
no deliverance for them.   But when they realise the
power and tyranny of that to which they have sold
themselves ; when they discover the havoc it is
playing with their constitutions, their minds, their
characters, and their futures ; when they see that it
is imperative for them to be set free ; and when they
wake up to the fact that they have no power to
recover themselves, and that they need a saviour ;

then if they cry to the Lord He will help them, and that right speedily.

These prayers of the children of Israel represent the lowest form of prayer, that is, of successful prayer. There are requests that strike a much lower note than these, but then such are not answered. "Ye ask and receive not because ye ask amiss."

These petitions are wholly for themselves. Their personal distress has called them forth. They do not pray for the sake of others, nor with any desire for the glory of God. The cry has been forced from them. Not until they could not help praying did they pray. They were in a corner. They had had no use for God when things seemed bright. They only came to Him when they could not do without Him. There was unmistakably an element of meanness in their attitude. Their cry was not for power with which to serve God, but simply for deliverance from a cruel bondage.

But all this that was in their prayers is in the prayers of most of us when first we begin to pray in earnest. Our first prayers are for ourselves. They are forced from us by some trouble. We have forgotten God, and given our heart and strength to our own interests and desires. When the fear of the harvest of our sins comes home to us, the fear of death and of judgment, we cry unto God. The first real prayers of many of us were selfish. A higher type comes later. Not until we are delivered do we begin to pray for others, and to long for God's name to be known and honoured. It is fear, and bondage, and trouble, that make us first cry out.

But it is this cry which God hears. He begins with us as we are. He does not wait until we have been raised to a certain level before He listens. He hearkens to our cry as sinners first. He makes us saints, and then we pray as saints. But in the first place it is the cry of the publican, "God be merciful to me a sinner," that is heard. And this is where the gospel comes in, and where there is hope for us all. If God would not help us until we were on a higher platform of desire than the selfish one, we never should be heard. We cannot get higher until God hears our prayer and delivers us from sin and self.

Let us notice what this cry of children of Israel included. *There was Confession.* They said : "We have sinned." And the confession was particular : "We have forsaken our God, we have served the Baalim." They knew wherein they had sinned, and they acknowledged their particular offence. The promise of forgiveness is preceded by the words, "if we confess our sins." It is not a general confession of sinnership that is required ; that is acknowledged by all ; but a particular confession of individual sinfulness.

This is not the first time these people had

acknowledged their transgressions.   They are back-sliders returning to God.   And return to God is not easy.   In this case the Lord said He would not hear them.   He said : " Did I not save you from the Egyptians, and from the Amorites, from the children of Ammon, and from the Philistines ?   The Zidonians also, and the Amalekites, and Maonites did oppress you ; and ye cried unto Me, and I saved you out of their hand.   Yet ye have forsaken Me, and served other gods ; wherefore I will save you no more.   Go and cry unto the gods which ye have chosen ;   let them save you in the time of your distress."   God practically told them that they had made a convenience of Him, and He was not going to have that done any more.   Let them go to those whom they were serving.   That was a perfectly fair proposition.   It is not so easy, after repeated falls, to come back to God as it is to come to Him in the first place.   The haunting fear of whether it will last, the remembrance of repeated failings, and the recollection that we have meant well before, but have not been able to continue, all hinder us.   Then repeated sinning makes us greater slaves to evil. Habits have become a part of us.   No ! it is not easy coming back to God after several falls.

And it ought not to be easy.   It is quite right that it should get harder, and that we should know it and feel it.   It will make us more careful, and make us feel that to slip again is only to add to the

difficulties of repentance.   If we get the idea that
God receives us as readily and easily each time, some
amongst us may be for ever sinning and repenting.
Forgiveness is wonderfully free on God's part, but
it is not easy.   Forgiveness is not an easy thing
with us, and it is not an easy thing with God.
Before the remission of sins could be preached as a
gospel to the whole world, it was necessary for Christ
to die.   It cost God His Son to make forgiveness
free to us.   We must not have light views concerning
the pardon of our sins.

But though it is harder to get back, return is
possible. *These people persevered.*   They said : " We
have sinned : do Thou unto us whatsoever seemeth
good unto Thee ; only deliver us, we pray Thee,
this day.   And they put away the strange gods from
among them, and served the Lord."   They valued
forgiveness and deliverance.   They became more
urgent.   And to their confession they added action.
They gave a guarantee of their genuineness in that
they gave up the things which were wrong ; and,
before deliverance came, they began to serve the
Lord.   That is the way the light breaks.   There are
evils that must be put away, and acts of obedience
rendered before assurance of acceptance can come
to the soul.   Repentance, surrender to Christ, and
confession of Him before men, must accompany
prayer.   Actions as well as plaintive speech are
required to show that |we are in earnest.   We

are to "bring forth fruits meet for repentance."

And the cry of the children of Israel moved God. "His soul was grieved for the misery of Israel." God is unchangeable, but He is not immovable like a rock. His heart can be touched. There are things that appeal to Him. Genuine repentance, distress, strong desire, these things touch Him, and He responds. He will not leave a true man alone. If you really are anxious to be better, and to be delivered, God will come to your aid. "Wilt thou be made whole," He says. "If any man will come after Me," "Whosoever will." Where there is a will God will find a way to bless. "Those that hunger and thirst after righteousness shall be filled."

III.

Under Samuel.

*" And Samuel spake unto all the house of Israel, saying :
If ye do return unto the Lord with all your hearts, then put
away the strange gods and Ashtaroth from among you, and
prepare your hearts unto the Lord, and serve Him only ; and
He will deliver you out of the hand of the Philistines."*—
1 SAMUEL vii. 3.

BOTH the religious and the national life of Israel
were at a low ebb. For years an old and
feeble priest had been at the head of affairs. His
sons ministered in the priest's office. They were
covetous and immoral, and used their position for
their own vile ends. The offerings of the Lord were
consequently abhorred. Their father, Eli, had not
the courage to deal with them as a parent should, or
to purify the service of the Lord's house, as the
position of high priest required him to do. The
service of God was neglected and in disrepute. At
this time the Philistines came against the people,
and inflicted upon them a severe defeat. In their
extremity the Israelites sent for the ark of God.
They did not inquire into the moral reasons why

the Lord's help was not forthcoming. They turned superstitiously to a symbol instead of to the living God. Their religion was one of externals only, and was altogether independent of questions of character. With the ark in their midst they fought another battle with the Philistines, but were defeated more disastrously than ever. The ark itself was taken, the priests were slain, and Shiloh, their national centre and the meeting place of their faith, was laid waste. For 20 years they were under the heel of the Philistines, and had no place where they gathered to worship God. Though the ark was returned by their oppressors, it was consigned to a private house. It was no longer a rallying point for their faith. Then the people began to lament after the Lord. They became conscious of His absence. There was a power and a blessing, once enjoyed, but now missed. The presence of the living God was their need.

How this yearning found expression we do not know, but we have, in our text, the answer that Samuel gave to their longing. The instructions were obeyed. With all their heart they sought and served the Lord. A national assembly was convened, and ceremonies, expressive of their contrition and of their whole-hearted surrender to God, were observed. They confessed their sins, and individual cases were judged by Samuel, and his judgments were accepted. Then the Philistines gathered against them again. Samuel prayed for deliverance ; and, before a blow was struck by them either in self-defence or for liberty, the power of the Lord was made manifest. In a thunderstorm He appeared and discomfited their foes. They saw that He was once more amongst them ; and, acting under the inspiration of this, they pursued their enemies and were delivered out of their hands. National deliverance followed a general revival of religious faith and practice. The points we will notice in this story are : The Cause, The Conditions, and The Consequences of Revival.

I.—THE CAUSE OF REVIVAL.

In our study of the revival under Moses in Egypt, we noticed that God is the great first, moving cause in such an event. That fact remains concerning all real religious awakenings. In this story we deal, however, with the secondary cause.

The human cause was Samuel. He was the instrument that God used. When quite a boy the Lord had spoken to him and given him His first message. This was one of warning and rebuke to Eli for the careless way in which he dealt with his family and supervised the Lord's work. After that " the Lord appeared again in Shiloh : for the Lord revealed Himself to Samuel in Shiloh by the word of the Lord. And the word of Samuel came to all Israel." That is the record of 20 years before the revival. But the work that produced the great awakening began then. Our text must not be regarded as an isolated utterance of the great prophet at the end of the twenty years, but as an epitome of the message which, during that period, he was continually giving. The burden of his preaching was that the reason for their defeat and oppression was moral. The nation would not revive until religion revived. If there was a widespread reformation in their lives the Lord would give them deliverance. For twenty years Samuel preached this. It took all that time for it to sink into their minds. But it bore its fruit at last. The revival seemed sudden when it came, but it was the result of years of patient labour. This is a lesson we need to learn.

A revival is sadly needed in this land. The religious life is low. Morality is conspicuous by its absence in much of our business life. Men have little conscience in the matter of debt. Gambling is indulged in to an alarming extent. Social evils grow. Not only are divorces on the increase, but the number of wives and families abandoned by their husbands is very great. An awakening that will touch the consciences of men is needed if religion is to be an aggressive force, and if our social, commercial and civic life is to be saved from ruin. With these facts before us, and encouraged by the Welsh Revival, we have begun to pray and work for revival. After a short time many have become discouraged. We see no great movement, and we think we have

expected too much.   We begin to explain that the
Revival in Wales is largely a matter of temperament,
that the people are emotional, and naturally religious.
We say it is impossible to have such a revival here.
Our circumstances are so different, our populations
are so mixed, we have such a mass of anti-Christian
element.   Judaism, Mahommedanism, Hindooism,
Confucianism—all number their adherents by the
thousand.   The emigrants from Continental Europe
have a lower moral standard than the British and
the Dutch, and a greater mixture of superstition with
their religion.   All these combine against the atmosphere that would issue in a revival.   But our God is
equal to all this.   The special difficulties are a
challenge to His power and to our faith.   The
greater the difficulty and the need, the greater the
reason for a revival.   But we must have patience.
We must be prepared to work long, and to do what,
in the political world, Lord Rosebery calls spade
work.   God's best things can only be given to those
who show appreciation of their value by persistent
desire and effort to obtain them.   The spasmodic
prayers that represent flitting desires, though they
are good, He does not answer.   The prayers which
reveal the settled longing of the heart are the prayers
He heeds.   And it takes time to reveal that such
desires are possessed by us.

Some may be inclined to say : " If we only had
a man like Samuel amongst us we should soon have

a revival. But we lack an outstanding leader."
Wales has given us the answer to this. The work
there is the work of no one man. God has used
many men, and many of humble origin. There is a
story told concerning the football team of Harvard
University which is also appropriate to this. For
several seasons the Harvard team was beaten by
those from the Yale and Pennsylvania Universities.
Three young men gave themselves to the task of
finding the cause, and also a remedy. The tide of
defeat was stayed, and then it turned to victory.
One day, after beating Yale by 28 to nil, a friend
enquired about the new plan, and received a reply to
the effect that every member of the old team was a
star. Each was the best in his own particular line,
and each played his own particular part, but the
playing was that of individuals. "Now," he said,
"we have only one star, but we have a team. We
all work together." Is there not in that a hint for
us? A number of us working together can equal a
Samuel. With faith in and consecration to God,
and with a conviction of the need of and desire for
revival, the blessing can come through us.

II.—THE CONDITIONS OF REVIVAL.

1. *Earnestness.*—"If ye do return unto the
Lord with all your hearts," said Samuel. That is, if
you are in earnest, then put away the strange gods.
Nothing that is required to bring revival can be done

unless, first of all, there be whole-heartedness. "If you mean business," Samuel seems to say, "I can give you the programme, but it turns upon this, 'If with all your hearts.'" But this earnestness that must precede everything else must continue throughout and permeate the remaining conditions. After putting away comes: "Prepare your hearts unto the Lord," or "set" or "make firm your hearts." Also "serve Him only." The whole thing must be done with the entire being.

John Collett Ryland, in the eighteenth century, at the age of 20, wrote these words: "If there is ever a God in heaven or earth, I vow and protest, in His strength, or that God permitting me, I'll find Him out; and I'll know whether He loves or hates me; or I'll die and perish, soul and body, in the pursuit and search." Ryland not only found God, but became one of His ministers. Within six years of writing this he was called to be the pastor of a Baptist church. Such earnestness cannot fail of finding God. "The kingdom of heaven suffereth violence, and the violent take it by force."

2. *Repentance.*—Though the people had forgotten God they had not altogether discarded religion. In the place of the true they had put the false. The false gods and the practices connected therewith must now be put on one side. Whilst the mind was occupied with other gods, the true God could not be seen. The heart must be wholly turned to Him to

see Him ; and in order to do this that which filled the vision must be put on one side. In this country we have not to face the substitution of a false religion for the true, so much as we have to face the substitution of the things of this life for the eternal. " The pure in heart shall see God." The reverse is true : " The impure shall not see Him." Lust blinds the eyes to God. Men cannot see Him, or be sure of Him, when they are lustful. It is easy and natural to be sceptical when impure.

Money is as blinding to the true vision as lust. If men are wholly occupied with the pursuit of wealth, and are determined upon getting money, they cannot see God. It is not a question so much of whether the methods of getting it are justifiable or unscrupulous, as it is the absorption in the pursuit of it. A man who has no time for anything else but business, though he run his business honestly, will find that God is outside his vision. His whole horizon is filled with that which absorbs him. Men must turn from the whole-hearted pursuit of money if they would get right with God.

Ambition is equally blinding. "How can ye believe," Christ said, "which receive honour one of another, and seek not the honour that cometh from God only ?" If the praise of our fellows be the dominant motive of our life we cannot find God. If we are prevented from taking our stand for Him, simply because it would mean the contempt of those

whose good will we value, we shall find it impossible
to be refreshed and helped by His presence. The
inspiring, comforting, purifying effect of His presence
is worth every sacrifice ; and anything that is first,
and places Him in a secondary position, must be
put on one side.

This repentance includes confession. The
children of Israel gathered at Mizpah and said :
" We have sinned against the Lord." The facts of
one's life must be faced. The sins must be acknowledged. The responsibility for them must be taken.
The blame must not be put upon circumstances.
True confession is accepting the guilt. " If we confess our sins He is faithful and just to forgive us
our sins."

But confession is not completed by making a
secret acknowledgment unto the Lord. If our sins
have been against individuals, and these are within
reach of our word, the confession must be made to
them. "Confess your faults one to another, and
pray one for another, that ye may be healed," says
James. "Samuel judged the children of Israel in
Mizpah." The individual cases came before him,
and wrongs were righted. Relationships that were
discordant were made harmonious. When people
are ready to make up their quarrels revival is not
far off.

III.—THE CONSEQUENCES OF REVIVAL.

1. *Unity.*—The Book of Judges concludes with

the sentence : " Every man did that which was right in his own eyes." There was no recognized head. Eli, as high priest, never rallied or united the people. Not till Samuel came was the old unity restored. Now "all the house of Israel lamented after the Lord." " Samuel spake unto all the house of Israel." "And Samuel said : Gather all Israel to Mizpah."

Revival always means unity. In Wales the churches have never been so one as at the present time. Though the distinctive rite of the Baptists has been more in evidence than ever, 40,000 out of the 80,000 converts having been publicly baptised, the harmony of the churches has not been disturbed. In spite of the fierce controversy over the Education Act, Church of England clergymen have joined with the ministers of the Free Churches in the meetings for prayer and the care of the converts. The points of agreement are seen to be more ; and whilst individual convictions are not lessened, they do not divide the workers.

In South Africa revival would mean not only greater unity amongst the churches, but amongst our various races. The great mission of Gipsy Smith brought together in the centres he visited men who had been separated for years, and that kind of thing would be multiplied throughout the land if revival should sweep over it like a great wave.

2. *Conflict.*—The children of Israel could not bestir themselves without their gathering appearing to be a challenge to the Philistines. Sooner or later the two powers must be pitted one against the other. Revival does not mean ease. It is a preparation for work. It will either arouse the organized forces of evil into open hostility, or it will compel the Christian forces to attack them more seriously.

3. *Deliverance.*—"And He will deliver you out of the hand of the Philistines." When the religious life of a country is low the wicked prosper, and at the expense of the majority of the people. Drinking corporations flourish, monopolies and trusts come to great estate, wealth is amassed without any consideration for those who are pushed on one side. Dividends have to be paid, and corporations are heartless. Revival means a great awakening of the public conscience, and with that awakening deliverance from greed and selfishness and corruption will follow.

IV.

Under Asa.

2 CHRON. XV.

A GREAT revival of religion took place in the fifteenth year of the reign of Asa, king of Judah. The awakening was different from any of those which we have already considered. It did not follow a period of religious decline, but an era of reformation. Neither was it occasioned by national adversity, causing the people in despair to turn to God; but it came after a season of increase and prosperity; and after a great national victory and deliverance. During the two preceding reigns, the worship of Jehovah had been pushed into the background, and the erection of idols, and places for their worship, had proceeded with the active support of the rulers. Upon Asa's accession ecclesiastical reform was immediately effected. The State policy was reversed. The people were commanded to observe the law of God, and an active campaign against idolatry was instituted. A period of quiet settled upon the land, and the freedom from external attack was utilized for internal develop-

ment and the strengthening of the national defences.
After ten years of progress, an army of one million
Ethiopians came against Judah. Asa took the field
with only half that number of soldiers. But Asa
"cried unto the Lord." And the Lord heard his
prayer and gave a mighty victory to His people. As
the king and his hosts returned, the prophet Azariah
met them and called their attention to the condition
of Israel during the times of the Judges, and to the
fact that whenever the people turned to God He
was found of them. Encouraged by the story of
the past and the exhortation of the prophet, the zeal
of Asa was quickened, and the work of reformation
was carried further still. There were some abuses
that had not yet been dealt with, and there were
works for God which had not been undertaken.
Following this increased zeal against the false faiths
and on behalf of the true, was the calling of a
national assembly at Jerusalem. The success which
had crowned Asa's reforming zeal in the early years,
the response made by God to his faith in the hour
of national danger, the further zeal following the
words of the prophet, all served to awaken the
religious spirit in the people. They came "to him
in abundance when they saw that the Lord his God
was with him." In the fifteenth year of his reign
Asa found his policy and example had borne fruit,
and that his subjects were thoroughly infected with
the spirit that animated him. "They entered into a

covenant to seek the Lord God of their fathers with all their heart and with all their soul." And in accordance with the law which said, "He that sacrificeth unto any god, save unto the Lord only, he shall be utterly destroyed," they determined that "whosoever would not seek the Lord God of Israel should be put to death." The revival was marked with great joy. The people "rejoiced at the oath, for they had sworn with all their heart, and sought Him with their whole desire." Asa also found another matter claiming his attention. The queen, Maacah, mother of the king, had erected an idol in a grove. This he destroyed, and Maacah he deposed. A further period of rest—this time of 20 years—marked the Lord's approval of the national awakening. This story shows—

I.—THAT REVIVAL IS POSSIBLE IN A TIME OF PROSPERITY.

The majority of the revivals of the Bible, and the majority of those in the Christian era, have followed periods of religious decline and of national trouble. It is with nations as with individuals—trouble is generally required to make them turn to the Lord. Not till we are in extreme case do we, as a rule, seek Him. And so it is possible for us to feel that revival cannot come without trouble. The statement has been frequently made about ourselves in South Africa that we have to be brought a good deal lower yet before any great blessing can come to us. It is true we have had a long spell of disastrous events, and that the spirit of our people is not yet one of deep humility before the Lord. If there is no great turning to the Lord we shall probably see more trouble and prolonged uncertainty. But there is nothing on God's side necessitating further chastisement. It is only human perversity that makes trouble a preliminary to blessing. The history of Asa shows that God's Spirit can work at all times. Other stories have told us that adversity is not a bar to revival. This one tells us that though prosperity is not generally conducive to it, it need not hinder it.

II.—Revival is helped by a Remembrance of the Past.

Azariah's address about former awakenings was a great stimulus to Asa. When he heard the prophecy he took courage. The prophecy was in the ancient story. What had been could be again. The history of the past is always possible in like conditions. In the time of the Judges—or rather in the period covered off and on by their rule, for their rule was spasmodic, not continuous—there had been great awakenings. The people were leaderless ; civil government was not established ; the work of God was unorganized ; every city was in danger of attack ; there was no security anywhere for life or property; and yet in such conditions the people had sought and found the Lord. If this were possible then, what was not possible now? They were strong; the throne was firmly established; the country was safe; preachers had liberty to give their messages; the priests had facilities for sacrifice; and the influence of the court was all on the side of good. The story of the past was certainly possible of repetition. And in this manner we should encourage ourselves to-day. We read of many awakenings in Old Testament times, in seasons of adversity and prosperity, with the help of the king, and sometimes with his influence on the opposite side. About sixteen revivals are recorded, or hinted at, between the times of Moses and Nehemiah. These awakenings occurred before the advent of Christ, before the knowledge of God and of His will was so clear as it is to-day, and before His Spirit was poured out as at Pentecost. How much more possible is revival for us? The conditions are far more favourable.

Then the history of revival in the Christian era is helpful. God has never been without witness. In the darkest ages men have stood up for Him, and won others too. When confession of Christ meant death, the preaching of the Word imprisonment, attendance at public worship and possession of the Scriptures the confiscation of goods, revivals occurred. Before freedom of conscience was established, before printing was invented, and when, after the invention of printing, the Bible was a dear book, and the common people could not read, in all these times religious awakenings took place. With the multiplication of Christian agencies and influence, and the widespread diffusion of the Scriptures, coupled with the abiding presence of the Holy Spirit, what wonderful seasons of refreshing may be ours.

The revival in Jonathan Edwards' church in America in the eighteenth century was occasioned by hearing of revival in England. The story of it in that church called forth prayerful and expectant effort in other quarters. The revival in Ireland and Wales in 1859 was helped by the story of a similar event in the United States in 1857, and the revival in Ireland and Wales led to a like work of grace in England and Scotland. The present awakening in Wales has already borne fruit in other lands ; and in this country the blessing we are expecting will be largely due to the prayerful interest with which that movement is being followed.

III.—Revival requires an Increase of Spiritual Life amongst those already possessing it.

Asa had taken a strong stand against evil ; he had put his hand with considerable energy to good things ; he had exhibited great faith in a time of trouble ; he had given evidence that he had learnt the art of successful prayer ; and he had been blessed so conspicuously that people saw that God was with him, and yet there was room for improvement. There were evils still tolerated in the country and in his home. And there were also works of God awaiting his hand. The altar of the Lord required renewal, and the dedicated things needed to be brought into the temple. And when Asa consecrated himself to these things God sent the blessing.

In an admirable book on " The Revival in Wales and some of its Hidden Springs," Mrs. Penn Lewis traces the awakening there to a series of conventions and meetings, in which good men and women entered into a deeper life. If the tone of the life of the members of our churches be considerably raised the blessing will not tarry. The great masses of the people are unreached by our church agencies. They will not come to our meetings ; but they are all touched during the week, in daily life, by Christian people. If in the midst of the world our spirit be different from its spirit, if there we are gentle, patient and forgiving, happy and contented, unselfish and loving, the masses will be brought face to face with personified Christianity. They will pause and consider its meaning. It will first rebuke them, and then in many cases it will win them. " The strangers out of Ephraim and

Manasseh and out of Simeon fell to Asa in
abundance, when they saw that the Lord his God
was with him." The outsiders were reached by the
deepening of his religious life.

IV.—REVIVAL NECESSITATES DRASTIC MEASURES WITH EVILS.

Idolatry is degrading to character and demoralizing to social life. It obscures God. The world
was so sunk in it that it was necessary for a people
to be called out from the world, separated from it,
and by strong laws and discipline purified from the
prevailing faith and practices, in order that the true
faith might be planted, preserved, and propagated.
The history of the Jews shows that idolatry could
not be dealt with on any other line but an intolerant
one. In the New Testament the firm and intolerant
attitude of the nation to evil is laid upon the individual. Habits which are as much a part of us as
hands and eyes are to be surgically treated if they
hinder the soul's growth. The power of God can
only flow through the man whose life is clearly and
definitely severed from sin. The same position
must be taken by the church. Her hands must be
free from everything that degrades the life of the
people. There are evils amongst us as demoralizing
as idolatry was amongst the Jews.

The drink is one of these. The terrible increase
of insanity, which is a national peril, is due to drink

more than to any other one cause. Crime, poverty, and disease each owes more to intoxicants than to any other single thing. The physique, the mental power, the wealth, the social life, the character and security of our people, are threatened by this terrible scourge. The church must not be afraid to be intolerant of it. We are told we must not interfere with the liberty of the subject. But the liberties of us all have been long interfered with through the freedom and licence granted to "the trade." The church should purge itself completely of the evil. No one interested in the liquor traffic should be elected to its sacred offices, and all should take the total abstinence position. Any other platform but the total abstinence one is ineffective for God's people to occupy.

Another evil sapping the best life of the country is gambling. The complete absorption of the masses of the people in sport—an absorption that means that in the time of national trouble the issue of a football or cricket match puts in the shade the issue of a battle or a campaign, an absorption that means that questions upon which the nation's future depends, and upon which each man is called to vote, are only seriously discussed by the few—is due not to the active participation of the people in the games themselves, but to the betting and sweepstakes connected therewith. And this interest means that the masses are financially and personally interested in the issue of each sporting event, and whilst the issue of these events is uncertain, the employer does not and cannot have the whole-hearted attention of his employees. The gambling spirit is against efficiency in business; and to men handling money it is a constant source of temptation. It fosters the spirit of dependence upon chance, and is a menace to honest, steady toil. Members of Christian churches should abstain from betting, sweepstakes, and playing for money in games of chance; and the churches in their corporate capacity should rigorously exclude all raffling, etc., from bazaars and sales of work. If the church allows these things, even "for a good cause," it cannot protest effectually against the evil.

V.—Revival calls for Courageous and Purposeful Effort.

The conqueror of a million, himself at the head of an army of half a million victorious soldiers, is urged to be strong, and told that his hands should not be weak. The courage of the battlefield fails in the presence of moral evil. A different spirit is wanted to stand against sin, especially when that sin is in one's own household. It did my heart good the other night to hear two or three strapping young men, who looked as if they would be afraid of no one, confessing their weakness to the Lord, and asking Him to give them courage to confess Christ before their comrades. "Even the youths shall

faint and be weary, and the young men shall
utterly fall ; but they that wait upon the Lord shall
renew their strength."

Asa not only needed courage but purpose. He
made up his mind to obey the Lord, and to work
for the blessing promised. There is need for Christians to consecrate themselves for the work of
revival. It will not come without definite purpose
on the part of some. Individuals must make up
their minds to live for this purpose, to study the
laws of revivals, and to work and pray wholeheartedly for blessing. With courageous and purposeful effort the work will be hastened.

V.

Under Elijah.

1 KINGS, xvii. and xviii.

IN the reign of Ahab and Jezebel the children of Israel were becoming confirmed in idolatry. For over fifty years the people had been departing from the old faith, until the worship of Baal had become the State religion. For the first time in their history their ancient faith was persecuted. Men worshipped Jehovah with their lives in their hands. The prophets of the Lord were hunted down and put to death. One hundred of them were saved through the help of Obadiah, a friend at court, who hid them in a cave and supplied them with bread and water. The people were contented with this state of things. The country was prosperous ; new towns were built ; large palaces, public buildings, and temples were erected ; and the prestige of the nation amongst the surrounding peoples was high.

One man, however, was studying his Bible. It was a small book compared with the one we have to-day. In it he found these words : " It shall come to pass, if ye shall hearken diligently unto My commandments which I command you this day, to love the Lord your God, and to serve Him with all your heart, and with all your soul, that I will give you the rain of your land in his due season, the first rain and the latter rain, that thou mayest gather in thy corn, and thy wine, and thine oil. And I will send grass in thy fields for thy cattle, that thou mayest eat and be full. Take heed to yourselves, that your heart be not deceived, and ye turn aside, and serve other gods, and worship them ; and then the Lord's wrath be kindled against you, and He shut up the heaven, that there be no rain, and that the land yield not her fruit ; and lest ye perish quickly from off the good land which the Lord giveth you." Under the influence of this, Elijah "prayed earnestly that it might not rain." It was an awful prayer, but he saw that if the people were to be won back to the faith of their fathers they must reap the consequences of their idolatry. They were not open to argument. They were utterly indifferent to the claims of God, and would not give them a moment's thought. It was imperative that they should find the way of transgressors to be hard ; and so Elijah prayed that God's Word might be fulfilled.

When he was sure that what the Lord had said would come to pass he publicly announced the course of events. In the court of the king he declared : "As the Lord God of Israel liveth, before whom I stand, there shall not be dew nor rain these years, but according to my word." And then under command from God he retired from public life.

For three and a half years the Word of God was not preached. There was a famine of the Word. And there was also another famine. The logic of events was to make its appeal to the people. A drought settled upon the country. The land gradually dried up. The sky, for month after month, remained a pitiless blue. The crops failed; the cattle and sheep pined away; the people sickened and died. Ahab had the country scoured in vain to find provision for his horses. Under the stress of these years a scapegoat had to be found, and Elijah was denounced as the cause of all the trouble. There was not a place known to the king to which he did not send for the prophet. A price was upon his head. But the judgment was doing its work. As the hearts of the people fainted within them they were being prepared to hear God's message. They were getting hungry for comfort and help; and when the time was ripe Elijah was bidden to show himself to Ahab. This he did. But the king had no power to arrest him. There was a power with him that made the king tremble in his presence. The subject commanded the ruler. Under the direction of Elijah, Ahab summoned a national assembly. The people gathered in their thousands, and Elijah appealed to the masses direct with his message. "How long," he said, "halt ye be-

tween two opinions ?   If the Lord be God,
follow Him ; but if Baal, then follow him."
To this there was no response.   "The people
answered him not a word."   Then he proposed a
test.   Two bullocks should be selected for sacrifice.
One should be prepared by the prophets of Baal,
the other by himself.   These should be placed on
altars with wood, but no fire.   "And," said the
prophet, "call ye on the name of your gods, and I
will call on the name of the Lord : and the god that
answereth by fire, let him be God."   To this the
people agreed.   The bullocks were brought, and the
prophets of Baal were given the first opportunity of
obtaining the desired effect.   For hours, in the
hottest part of the day, with the burning rays of the
sun shining upon their offering, these men, 450 in
number, arrayed in all the paraphernalia of their
office, careered and danced around their altar, crying,
"O Baal, hear us ! O Baal, hear us !"   Tricks were
impossible in the daylight, and under the eyes of
such a multitude.   As the hours dragged on the
excitement rose, and in their frenzy they jumped
upon the altar, cried aloud, and cut themselves with
knives.   But "there was neither voice, nor any to
answer, nor any that regarded."

Then Elijah called the people near to him.
The altar of the Lord, which was broken down, was
repaired ; the sacrifice was made ready ; the wood
was saturated with water ; over the whole water was

poured three times, and the trench surrounding the altar was filled. Then Elijah prayed : " Lord God of Abraham, Isaac, and of Israel, let it be known this day that Thou art God in Israel, and that I am Thy servant, and that I have done all these things at Thy word. Hear me, O Lord, hear me ; that this people may know that Thou art the Lord God, and that Thou hast turned their heart back again." And he did not pray in vain. The fire of the Lord fell, and " when all the people saw it, they fell on their faces, and they said, The Lord, He is the God ; the Lord, He is the God." The people returned *en masse* to the God of their fathers. The prophets of Baal were destroyed. The national repentance was complete.

But as yet there was not a speck in the sky. The heavens continued to be as brass. But the people had repented, and Elijah once more publicly committed God. He declared that there was the sound of abundance of rain ; and with that promise ringing in their ears the people returned to their homes. Elijah's work, however, was not complete. Though the promise of God was so absolute, and so certain of fulfilment, it needed human co-operation to make it effective. " Thus saith the Lord God, I will yet for this be inquired of by the house of Israel to do it for them." Elijah retired to pray, and as earnestly as he had requested that it might not rain, so now he prayed that the showers might fall. And when a cloud no bigger than a man's hand appeared in the sky he sent word at once to Ahab to hasten home before the storm broke.

On the surface of the story Elijah appears to us as a man of gigantic character, and quite impossible of imitation. But the Apostle James assures us he " was a man subject to like passions as we are." There were moments when he exhibited cowardice, faint-heartedness, and hopelessness, as we are prone to do. His greatness was due to that which is possible to us all—faith and prayer.

Elijah believed in the living God. "As the Lord God of Israel liveth before Whom I stand." This he said in the presence of Ahab. When he was before the whole court the most real being to him was God. He lived his life and uttered his words in the presence always of the King of Kings. To Him he was responsible. And this faith he had in an atmosphere similar to the one in which we live and work during the week. God is not real to the people of this land. He is not in all their thoughts. Business and pleasure absorb, and are realities; but God is far away. The complete banishment of God from the thoughts of the majority creates an atmosphere that affects our faith and our spiritual perceptions. In such an atmosphere Elijah also moved. But he came to it from another one. In retirement he had fellowship with God, he pondered over His words, he allowed them to sink into his soul till they governed his desires and thoughts. His inner life was brought into harmony with the revealed will of God. And after breathing this atmosphere for hours he could move amongst men and be unaffected by the air they breathed. His spiritual health was such that the diseased ideas of men could not impregnate him. When the presence of God is cultivated it becomes an overpowering, mastering sense, and with it a man moves victoriously amongst his fellows. It is not belief in the being of God that is our need, nor the furnishing of the mind with arguments for His existence ; but the sense of God, of His presence, of His sympathy and imminent help, and of our responsibility to Him. Such a feeling will enable us to act independently of the fear of man, and will make us strong.

Elijah believed in the Word of God. He had no doubts about its truth. What God had said would come to pass. His words were not idle ones. His promises and threatenings were equally true. The latter were righteous and necessary. It was not vindictiveness, nor delight in human misery, that caused God to threaten, but love for the souls of men. The threatenings were warnings. Their fulfilment was to turn men back to Him. "That they may know that Thou hast turned their hearts back again." This word needed to be received by men. It called them to co-operate with God for its fulfilment. It was a guide. It contained a programme. To this programme human acquiescence was necessary. Men must consent to it as good and just. The will revealed in it was a will to be accomplished through men. It was made known in order to bring men into line with God. So, accepting the word, and loving the people and the honour of God, Elijah prayed that, until their hearts were right they might know the bitterness of sin. The absence of rain was terrible, but contentment in a state of sin was a greater calamity. And when the people were broken under the influence of the drought he prayed again that rain might come.

God's Word abides. Such a faith as Elijah's we require. The programme of the Bible should be studied by us. To it we should agree. The revealed will of God should be our delight. For the realization of the promises we should pray and work.

This faith governed Elijah's life. It gave him courage to face Ahab and to tell him the truth. It enabled him to preach judgment to a people who did not believe in such a thing, and to whom such a doctrine was repugnant. He believed in the mercy of God to an unthinking, rebellious nation. God was more anxious to give rain than to withhold it. His faith enthused him, and he desired to communicate it. The people needed it. He desired they should understand and receive it. Prayer, hard work, earnestness, clear teaching, strong, loving desire, were born of such convictions. He could not help preaching. Such truths as he held with such intensity could not be bottled up. They must find expression. And the faith that enthused him was contagious. Men could not help feeling its power. It swayed the people. And though in some quarters it did not convince, it triumphed. It bore down the opposition of unbelief, and was found to be unanswerable. His faith, and not the unbelief of Ahab, ruled the people.

Such a faith, fed by the Word of God, and fostered in hours of retirement, is possible to us, and will make us instruments of revival to the people amongst whom we dwell.

VI.

Under Jonah.

JONAH was a prophet of Israel some eight centuries before Christ. He is the successor of Elisha at a distance of about eighty years. He is the first of the prophets whose utterances and work have a separate book devoted to them. Though occupying the tenth place in the prophetic Scriptures, the chronological position of the Book of Jonah should be first, coming before Isaiah.

My purpose is to deal with the revivals, and not with the question of the historical truth of the record. But I am aware that one cannot well enforce the lessons if the story itself is not believed to be true. So I will indicate a few lines of thought and study for the consideration of those who have their doubts.

First, the Book is endorsed by Christ. He refers to its events as actual history, and finds in it a type of His resurrection. He said : " An evil and adulterous generation seeketh after a sign ; and there shall no sign be given to it, but the sign of the prophet Jonas : for as Jonas was three days and three nights in the whale's belly, so shall the Son of man be three days and three nights in the heart of the earth." The Apostle Paul tells us that Christ "rose again the third day according to the Scriptures." The only Scripture that seems clear on the point of the third day is the word quoted by Christ concerning Jonah. It is replied that Christ only quoted Jonah as we would quote the characters from the Pilgrim's Progress. But Jonah is an historic character. We read of him in the books of the Kings. And Jesus refers to Jonah's converts as still having an existence, for they are to appear in the judgment. "The men of Nineveh shall rise in judgment with this generation, and shall condemn it ; because they repented at the preaching of Jonas, and behold, a greater than Jonas is here."

Second, the message of the Book is an inspired one. It is full of the mercy of the Lord. There is mercy to Jonah, to the sailors, to the Ninevites, their children and their cattle. It is a record of God's love far beyond the bounds of Israel. Its message was one no Israelite could have invented. Whether written 800 B.C. or 400 or 500 B.C., as we are now asked to believe, the same statement applies. Not till after Pentecost did Jewish thought rise to the actual preaching of God's love to the Gentiles, and even then the thought was of God. After the resurrection, the Great Commission of Christ, and Pentecost itself, the Apostles did not think of preaching to other than to Jews. A series of remarkable providential events is recorded in the

Book of the Acts as forcing the early church to extend a welcome to Gentile converts. The book of Jonah is far ahead of its time, and its message can only be accounted for by accepting it as inspired ; and if inspired it is impossible it would be enclosed in a lie.

Third, the discoveries of Archæology confirms its description of Nineveh. Because Strabo, Diodorus and Ptolemy, historians who lived before Christ, made no mention of the city, men argued that there could not possibly have been such a place. Tom Paine said about 130 years ago : "I don't believe a word of this story of great Nineveh." But in 1841, after having been buried for over 2,500 years, it was re-discovered, and the excavations in and around it shew that it occupied the tremendous area ascribed to it in the Book of Jonah. The reason why the historians referred to make no mention of it was because it was destroyed 500 years before either of them lived, and the memory of it had passed from men.

Fourth, the facts of natural history go a long way towards supporting the story of Jonah being swallowed by a fish. The cachalot whale and the white shark have been known in many instances to swallow men entire ; and, 24 hours after the cutting up of the fish has begun, men have been found inside, unconscious, but alive. Men fully dressed, their clothing untorn, horses, sea-calves as large as an ox, have been found in the stomach of sharks, sea-dogs and sperm-whales. Ordinarily digestion would have done its work on Jonah in three days ; but over against that possibility we have to set this fact : although the gastric juice is a remarkably powerful solvent, capable of dissolving many solid substances, yet it has no power whatever over living things. Jonah must die before digestion could even begin. I have said the facts of natural history go a long way towards supporting the story. I do not claim that these facts altogether verify it. That would be to eliminate the miraculous. But with these facts before us, plus God, the record becomes quite credible.

Coming now to the stories of revivals, we find a record of two, one amongst the sailors in the boat, and the other amongst the inhabitants of Nineveh. These stories are unique in the Old Testament. They are the only records of revivals amongst the heathen. All the other revivals we have considered have been Jewish. Jonah is the first foreign missionary in the Scriptures. But these stories are unique in another way. This is the first and only time in the Bible where the prophet's heart was not in his work. The rule is for God's evangelistic work to be done through men whose hearts echo His loving purposes of grace. But Jonah did not want his hearers to be converted. Let us consider :

I.—THE REVIVAL IN THE BOAT.

Jonah was running away from the Lord. He had been commanded to go to Nineveh, and to cry against it. But Jonah went to Joppa and found a ship going to Tarshish. So he paid the fare thereof that he might go in it from the presence of the Lord. When subsequently Nineveh was converted he gives the reason for his flight. "I fled unto Tarshish : for I knew that Thou art a gracious God, and merciful, slow to anger, and of great kindness, and repentest Thee of the evil." He could not bear the thought of the saved Nineveh. Nineveh was the capital of Assyria ; and to the inspired Seers of Israel it was becoming apparent that Assyria was to be God's instrument in the chastisement of his people. The overthrow of Nineveh, which without repentance was certain, meant a postponement of Israel's destruction. So Jonah's patriotism triumphed over his love for God's will.

This anti-missionary spirit is not dead yet. For centuries the priests were afraid to let the people have the Bible lest they should know as much as they. The spread of Scripture knowledge amongst the people meant the numbering of the days of the priests. Governing classes have opposed education lest the people should cease to be content to be serfs. The same spirit animates much of the opposition to missionary work. The conversion of the Kafirs makes it impossible to treat them as slaves. Education and conversion spoil the labour market for the sweaters. A Christianised Japan and China mean commercial rivalry for the white races.

But Jonah was not allowed to run away from his work. A storm pursued him. This was of such an extraordinary character that the sailors were sore afraid. They lightened the ship, and they prayed unto their gods, but all to no effect. Then they cast lots to see for whose cause the evil was upon them, and the lot fell upon Jonah. He told his story to them and they were awed. Here was a man whom a god was pursuing. Their sympathies were with him, and though he had told them to cast him into the sea, they rowed hard to bring him to the land. But the storm was against them. At last they felt that Jonah's word must be obeyed. It was their only chance. But they could not throw him overboard until they had prayed, and until they had committed themselves into God's hands. To Jehovah they cried. They could see He was a just God. He was one to be obeyed. His favourites had no dispensation to do as they pleased. But if He was strict for obedience would He not also acquit ? And so these heathen men rose to the thought of the Lord's justice being not of a vindictive but of a justifying character. They prayed that they might not perish for Jonah's sake, and that innocent blood might not be laid upon them. When the sea was calm again these men sacrificed unto the Lord and paid their vows. Their conversion outlived the storm. The fear of the Lord remained with them when the trouble was passed. Jesus said : " The men of Nineveh shall rise in the judgment with this generation and shall condemn it because they repented at the preaching of Jonas : and, behold a greater than Jonas is here." That same reasoning can be applied from the conduct of the sailors. These sailors shall rise in the judgment with this generation and shall condemn it because they believed when they saw the disobedience of Jonah, whilst the men of this age scoff when they witness the inconsistent conduct of Christians. They did not argue from Jonah's disobedience against God, but they found in it a reason for faith. Here was a God whose commands were to be taken seriously. Disobedience brought disaster to the disobedient one, and to all who happened to be in the same boat with him. By the nature of things the storm could not reach Jonah without involving his fellow passengers. We are members one of another, and we cannot sin, and reap the penalty alone. If to-day some prominent Christian man belies the trust reposed in him and comes to ruin and brings others down with him, the event is the occasion for much scoffing at the Christian faith. Such reasoning is superficial. The disaster is confirmatory of God's Word and not against it. "God is not mocked, for whatsoever a

man soweth, that shall he also reap." " The way
of transgressors is hard," whether the man be inside
or outside the visible Church.

II.—The Revival in Nineveh.

The second time the word of the Lord came to
Jonah he was not disobedient.   He went to Nineveh
and proclaimed : " Forty days and Nineveh shall be
overthrown."   This was doubtless only his text.
But the result of his preaching was remarkable.
The moral miracle is far beyond the physical one
recorded in this book.   There is no other case in the
Bible where the preaching of one man turned a
whole city, from the least to the greatest, to the Lord
in such a short space of time.   But this was a figure
of the pouring out of the Spirit upon all flesh, and
of nations being born in a day, experiences that in
the ages to come are to be common.

The revival was decidedly of the Lord.   It was
not born in any man's heart.   But, though of God,
he did not bring it to pass without preaching and
without a human agent.   God would have mercy
upon the city, but the call to repent must be given
through His appointed channel.   He has given to
His people the work of proclaiming repentance and
remission of sins.   If they do not do it it remains
undone.   The spirit bade Philip join himself to the
chariot of the Ethiopian eunuch ; and Philip, not
the Spirit, opened up to him the Scriptures.   Jesus

revealed Himself to Saul of Tarsus on the way to Damascus ; but in response to the question, " What wilt thou have me to do ? " Saul was directed to the city where it would be told him what he should do. And Ananias, not Christ, declared unto him the way of pardon, and the condition for receiving the Holy Spirit. The angel came to Cornelius to tell him that his prayer was heard. But he must send for Peter who would tell him words whereby he might be saved, he and his house. Neither the Holy Spirit, Jesus Christ, nor the angels, take out of men's hands the work of evangelizing which has been committed to them.

Our responsibility to the Great Commission of Christ is tremendous. The work of preaching is committed to the whole body, and there are people to-day in the same danger that Nineveh was in, in the days of Jonah's disobedience, because some of us are neither preaching the gospel ourselves, nor making it possible for others to preach it.

VII

Under Hezekiah.

2 CHRON. xxix., xxx., xxxi.

THE revival in the time of Hezekiah is amongst the most sudden of those recorded in the Scriptures. Hezekiah began a work of reformation during the first month of his reign, and within two months the whole land was swept with a wave of spiritual enthusiasm. The cause of such a sudden response on the part of the people is not directly stated, though a study of the times reveals some of the forces that prepared for such a movement. For 16 years under Ahaz, the preceding king, the country had been given over to idolatry. Those years were full of disaster ; and the series of troubles had no doubt a chastening effect upon the nation.

The ministries of three prophets were contemporary during this period. Isaiah was a prophet for a part of Uzziah's reign, and throughout the reigns of Jotham, Ahaz, and Hezekiah. In his book there is no record of a great religious awakening. His name is coupled with Hezekiah's in connection with events subsequent to the revival : but during the revival itself we have no hint of his presence. One cannot read his book, however, without feeling that such earnest preaching must have made some contribution towards the popular response to Hezekiah's reforming work. Hosea was a prophet whose words were uttered during the reigns of Uzziah, Jotham, Ahaz, and Hezekiah. His preaching was full of the national apostasy and the consequent troubles, and was urgent in its appeal for return. The last chapter of his book gives both the conditions and the promise of revival. The prophet Micah was equally plain in his statements and earnest in his pleadings. His ministry was exercised during the reigns of Jotham, Ahaz, and Hezekiah. Never in the whole course of Old Testament history were such a faithful and brilliant set of preachers contemporary as during this time. Though neither of them is mentioned in connection with the revival under Hezekiah, we cannot but conclude that their work was a powerful predisposing cause.

When Hezekiah came to the throne the temple was closed, its services discontinued, and much of its furniture thrown away. In the first month of his reign he assembled the priests and Levites, and addressed them on the causes of the troubles which had visited the land, and which he said were due to their departure from the living God. It was in his heart to make a covenant with the Lord that His wrath might be turned away. And to this end he desired to re-open the temple and to re-establish the worship of Jehovah. Fourteen Levites are named as the leaders in the work of cleansing the neglected shrine. These assembled their brethren. With the priests they must have constituted a body of men numbering several dozen. This considerable company was engaged for sixteen days in removing debris and finding and repairing the discarded furniture. When the work was completed, Hezekiah arranged for a great opening service. The rulers of the city, the priests, the Levites, and the inhabitants of Jerusalem, gathered in large numbers. The first ceremony was the sacrificing of a sin-offering for the kingdom, the sanctuary, and for Judah. This was an acknowledgment of transgression, and an appeal to God for forgiveness. Then—though the kingdom of Judah was separated from that of Israel, and though quite recently a terrible war had been waged between them, in which 120,000 men of Judah had been killed, and 200,000 men and women had been taken captive—a sin-offering for all Israel was made, the people thereby including their enemies in their prayer for pardon. Following this was the burnt-offering, which was expressive of their whole-hearted surrender to the will of God. Accompanying the burnt-offering was a service of song of a very hearty character. The Welsh revival has been described as a singing one. Such a description could be better applied to this revival under Hezekiah than to any other in the Old Testament.

Thank-offerings were next invited from the people. These came in so freely, and in such quantities, that it was soon evident the movement was more than an ecclesiastical reformation instituted by the king. The people were ready to return to the Lord. "And Hezekiah rejoiced, and all the people, that God had prepared the people : for the thing was done suddenly."

Such a work of grace could not be confined to the capital. As the result of taking counsel with the congregation, Hezekiah was enabled to send an invitation to all Israel and Judah to gather in Jerusalem to keep the Passover. Letters were prepared, and postmen despatched to every part of the country. The reception of the messengers was a mixed one. The majority in Israel laughed them to scorn and mocked them, but a considerable minority humbled themselves to respond. In Judah itself there was no division. "The hand of the Lord was to give them one heart to do the commandment of the king, and of the princes, by the word of the Lord." The largest assembly that had gathered in Jerusalem to keep the Passover since the days of Solomon was the result. A preliminary work of destroying the altars of sacrifice and incense erected unto the false gods was performed, and then the people settled down for seven days to the programme of confession, worship, sacrifice, and feast, prescribed by the law. The days were so full of power, blessing, and gladness, that without any hint from the king the people decided to continue another week ; so altogether fourteen days of services were celebrated.

The enthusiasm continued after the people had returned to their homes. In every centre to which they went back there were images, groves, high places and altars awaiting the attention of the iconoclasts ; and the work of destruction was thoroughly done. Word followed from the king that the tithes should be brought in. The response to this was tremendous. It showed how deep the work amongst the people was. A tenth of every-thing was speedily forthcoming. For four months a stream of live-stock and produce poured into Jerusalem. The most liberal provision was thereby made for the priests and Levites. The contributions were laid in heaps, and the king was summoned to see the result. "And when Hezekiah and the princes came and saw the heaps, they blessed the Lord, and His people Israel." Special chambers had to be prepared for the reception of the offerings, and men set apart to supervise the work of distribution. Diligent inquiries were set on foot, and provision was made, not only for the city priests, but for those in the country. The wives and children were also thought of ; and the burden of care was lifted from every priestly household in the land.

I.—THIS REVIVAL WAS ACCORDING TO THE WORD OF THE LORD.

In the Book of Deuteronomy the following instruction is written concerning the king : " And it shall be, when he sitteth upon the throne of his kingdom, that he shall write him a copy of this law in a book out of that which is before the priests the Levites : and it shall be with him, and he shall read therein all the days of his life : that he may learn to fear the Lord his God, to keep all the words of this law and these statutes to do them." Though we have no record of Hezekiah making a copy of the law, we have abundant evidence that he was thoroughly versed in its contents. That he knew the Book of Exodus we gather from his first address to the priests and Levites, in which he refers to the fact that God had chosen them to stand before Him. Other portions of the same address are an echo of the language of Deuteronomy concerning the consequences of apostasy. The arrangements for the Passover presuppose acquaintance with the Book of Numbers. The time for the celebration of this event was fixed for the first month ; but this date was passed before even word could reach the people to observe it. In the Book of Numbers (chap. ix.) provision is made for the observance of this great event, in case any special circumstances hindered its observance at the proper time. Of this provision Hezekiah now availed himself. The details given of the purification of the temple, the sanctification of the priests, the order and character of the offerings, the gifts of the people, all tell of familiarity with the Book of Leviticus. The knowledge of the law is further revealed in the king's anxiety and prayer, when it was found that some of the people from the farthest districts had, through ignorance, not been cleansed according to the purification of the sanctuary. The programme outlined in Deuteronomy xii. was literally observed. Other books of Scripture had by Hezekiah's time been added to the books of the law. The Book of Psalms had been partly composed; and the songs of David and Asaph were given a prominent place in the temple service.

The revival we need to-day is one according to the Word of the Lord. The promise of revival is definite, and can be realised whenever the conditions are fulfilled. God's laws of seed-time and harvest have been learnt by men through long experience and diligent study of Nature. The laws of revival are as certain; but they call for diligent and prayerful research. If we give ourselves to be familiar with them, and whole-heartedly comply with them, we shall find that blessing will speedily come.

Hezekiah was obedient to the Word of the Lord, as spoken by His servant Moses. In his time the laws of Moses had not been superseded. Christ has since set many of them on one side. He now is our Lawgiver, and our duty is to Him. There has been no revelation making any of His precepts obsolete. " Last of all He sent unto them His Son." " God hath in these last days spoken unto us in His Son." Careful attention to the words of Christ, and a loving obedience to the same, will assuredly bring revival.

II.—Revival means Increased Attendance at Public Worship.

Before Hezekiah began to reign the temple was closed. Revival began with its re-opening ; it was characterized by large congregations for worship ; and the work continued by means of pressing invitations, from the worshippers, to others to join.

Our places of worship are not closed, but they are neglected. The majority of the people are outside. A church census here would reveal a more lamentble state of things than the returns taken in some of the principal centres at home. Men tell us they can worship God by the seaside and on the mountain slopes. Of course they can ; but do they ? At present we have a revival of Sunday picnics and sports ; but such things do not tell in favour of character and general righteousness. Man is a social being, and his social characteristics are clearly evidenced by the results of observance or neglect of public worship. Assembling with others has a stimulating effect upon our spiritual life. Public worship brings to our minds truths and facts which we are too apt to forget in the rush of life. These have a corrective influence upon us. Regular worship helps to keep us up to the mark, and the life of the heart is thereby purified, renewed, and strengthened.

Under the influence of truths presented to us at worship we realize not only our own needs, but also those of others, and an interest in their spiritual welfare is created. The congregation at Jerusalem, after making confession and prayer for themselves, awoke to the needs of their fellows in the kingdom of Israel. Confession and prayer were then offered for them ; and this bore fruit in a desire to invite them to share in the blessings of the temple services. The results of public worship go beyond the well-being of the immediate worshippers. It is an institution which saves people from being self-centred ; it widens their interest in their fellows, and issues in activity on their behalf.

III.—Revival means that the Financial Needs of God's Work will be met.

The temple exchequer was the last thing to feel the influence of the revival ; but it was eventually affected by it, and in a substantial manner. One sure proof that the work of God has little hold upon the people is the constant poverty of the churches. There is an impression amongst some that these bodies are wealthy corporations. The constant proposal to appeal for a collection on behalf of needy causes bears this out. But there are no surplus collections to spare. The members may be rich, but the churches themselves are not. The unceasing stream of bazaars and sales of work is proof that the giving of the people is altogether inadequate for the carrying on of God's work. The evils attendant upon these means of raising money are constantly acknowledged, but they are defended on the ground that they are necessary evils. If the people gave according to their means, proportionately and systematically, there would be no need for the energies and enthusiasm of church members to be diverted from the spiritual and soul-saving work for which they exist to the work of raising money. If the people receive rich spiritual blessings from God, they will count it a privilege to support His work. The giving will be cheerful and liberal ; and financial anxiety will not hamper the efforts of the workers.

VIII.

Under Josiah.

2 CHRON., xxxiv. and xxxv.

JOSIAH began to reign over Judah when he was eight years of age. At 16 he began to seek the Lord; and at 20 he was sufficiently confirmed in his decision to be able to inaugurate an active campaign against idolatry. During the two preceding reigns, which lasted for nearly 60 years, the country had been given over to image-worship, and God's house had been closed and neglected. As this state of things continued during the early part of Josiah's reign, until the regency ended, it made altogether about 70 years of idolatry, a period long enough for the alien systems of faith to obtain a strong hold upon the people. Groves and high places and images were everywhere. For six years Josiah pursued his iconoclastic policy. At the same time an active propaganda on behalf of the temple was carried on, and large sums of money were collected. When he was 26 the work of repairing the temple was taken in hand. It was in this year, the eighteenth of his reign, that reformation issued in revival. With the exception of a very short interval at the end of Manasseh's reign, the temple had been closed for 75 years. The last religious awakening had taken place more than a century ago.

In connection with the cleansing of the temple, the most remarkable incident was the discovery of the book of the law. This was found by Hilkiah the priest, who gave it to Shaphan the scribe, who in his turn read it to the king. Its contents were news to Josiah, upon whom the reading had a marvellous effect. When he heard what God would do to His people if they forsook Him and followed other gods, his concern was great. He rent his clothes and wept. He directed the high priest and others to make inquiries concerning the fulfilment of the threats contained in the law. These went to Huldah the prophetess, who replied that the prophecies would certainly be fulfilled, but not in Josiah's time, as his heart was tender, and he had humbled himself at the reading of the Word. Then the king summoned the people to the temple, where he stood and read the law to them. If the book discovered was, as some suppose, only the Book of Deuteronomy, the reading to the king and by the king would have taken from three to four hours each.; but if it were the whole book of the law, some ten to twelve hours would have been occupied. In any case the time was longer than modern audiences are prepared to grant for such a purpose. At the conclusion of the reading Josiah publicly made a covenant with the Lord to obey all the words of the book, and urged the people to a like promise, to which they agreed. Then followed a further work of destruction. We have noticed before that though a man may have made a magnificent stand for the right, yet when he reads the Word of God he finds a good deal remaining to be accomplished. And this Josiah and his people found now. After the remaining abominations of the heathen had been removed, the Passover was celebrated. This quite eclipsed the observance in Hezekiah's time. The chronicler of that event had to go back to Solomon's reign to find its equal; but the historian of Josiah's Passover had to go back further still—to the time of Samuel—before he could find a feast as great.

Before dealing with the special lessons of this event, I desire to refer to one or two impressions left upon one's mind as the result of the continuous reading of these Old Testament stories of revival. This makes the thirteenth religious awakening amongst the Israelites. First of all was the revival in Egypt, which issued in the Exodus. Then followed a period of decline, necessitating forty years' wandering in the wilderness. Though no special revival meetings are noted, we know that faith was awakened at the end of this period to warrant the entry of the people into the promised land. During the rule of the Judges, five seasons of backsliding and return are chronicled. Then comes the awakening under Samuel, followed by a relapse under Saul. Faith was in the ascendant during the greater part of David's and Solomon's time, but decline set in towards the end of the latter's reign. When the kingdom divided into Israel and Judah, the apostasy of the former was checked for a time by the revival under the influence of Elijah ; and the slower decline of Judah was broken by revivals in the reigns of Asa, Hezekiah, and Josiah.

The first impression conveyed by this record is *the continued tendency of man to relapse.* The Fall of Man is not confined to the third chapter of Genesis. It is a continuous event. The world had a new start after the Flood ; the children of a righteous man being the progenitors of the new race. The righteousness of Noah was not transmitted by any hereditary law to his descendants ; and the warnings of the Flood seem to have been speedily forgotten. God then called Abraham and set him and his seed apart ; made Himself known to the patriarch and his descendants ; isolated them by rigorous laws from the rest of mankind ; gave a unique revelation to them; manifested Himself in miraculous deliverances and by special visible signs, such as the pillars of cloud and of fire ; taught the people by means of sacrifice and tabernacle service; gave them prophets who delivered unto them His Word; and enforced His laws by giving continuous blessing to obedience and unfailing want to disobedience. But even this nation fell again and again. The whole world was fallen; and the specially-favoured people showed the same general downward tendency. In the Christian era the same inclination is in evidence. Christ has come; the Holy Spirit has been given; the Church has been formed; the Bible completed; and yet men continue to relapse. The Fall is seen in the Church itself. "Back to Christ" is a cry which implies that the Church has not given its witness in a clear and unmistakable manner. The truths and commands of Jesus are corrupted or obscured by His own people. The Church has continually lapsed into pagan practices, or into indifference to the needs of men, or into unbelief about God's Word. Man's natural movement is not upwards. He corrupts the best things. Left to himself, all the goodness which has been granted to him speedily disappears. The advances which have been made have not been due to inherent aspirations and to unaided efforts, but to direct acts of God. God has repeatedly stepped in and arrested the Fall, and Himself provided the incentives and power for an upward move.

The second thought arises out of the first, and that is *the infinite patience and mercy of God.*

He will not let man fall for ever. Though he seems bent on decline, God steps in and arrests him. Faith in, obedience to, and knowledge of God are kept alive by influences started by God Himself for the purpose of calling men from their sins to righteousness. Were it not for repeated revivals, faith would die out, and character would go to ruin. This is our hope whenever faith is low. History shows that God will not give men up. He does not leave us to our own will and suffer us unhindered to go to our own destruction. Faith will never become extinct. God will visit and revive us before such a catastrophe occurs. If I saw no sign of awakening around us, if things were visibly to go from bad to worse, I should still believe in the prospect of revival.

Coming now to the story of Josiah, I desire to call attention to

I.—His Conversion.

He was 16 when he began to seek the Lord. What led him to do this we do not know. His father died when he was eight, but his father was a wicked man. His grandfather had been penitent in his old age ; but as Josiah was only five-and-a-half when Manasseh died he could not have been much influenced by him. There were no religious services for him to attend. The Bible of the day was lost. Those who taught him only knew its contents

second-hand. They had not seen the book themselves. In their younger days they may have been
taught by someone who once had seen and learnt
its contents. Its teachings were a tradition and a
memory, yet sufficient was known to awaken in
Josiah a desire to seek the Lord. God is found of
those that seek Him ; and in the course of time
Josiah found the Word, which was a great help to
a more perfect knowledge of God. The discovery
of the law must be regarded as a Divine act by
which God responded to Josiah's search. But
during the years of seeking the young king must
have made many mistakes. He must have held
many heretical and harmful notions. His concep-
tion of God could not possibly be very clear. When
he did find the Word, though then he had been
serving the Lord for many years, he was surprised
to find what a number of things were wrong. He
was humbled by the discovery of the evils still
requiring to be rectified. Things which had not
appeared to him as bad were now seen to be in-
tolerable. But all the mistakes of thought, and all
the wrong actions during the years of comparative
ignorance, did not prevent him from finding the
One he sought.

We are not in Josiah's position to-day. We
have a much fuller Book to guide us. But the Book
itself may be obscured by interpretations and teachings which have been given to us from our earliest

years. We read the Bible through the spectacles of our first teachers, and through the standards and creeds of our churches. There are truths that we need which those who taught us may not have seen, and in fact may have denied. If the teaching we have had has taken no cognizance of the need and possibility of the new birth ; if it has said nothing about the duty and character of repentance ; if it has not pointed us to the death of Christ as a death for our sins ; if it has not taught us the possibility of rejoicing in the full assurance of a present salvation, we shall not at first see these truths even though they are so plainly written in a Book which is in the hands of us all. But however obscured the true teaching may be on account of our training, the light will come to the man who seeks.

But though Josiah had ignorance as a hindrance, there was one great obstacle which he had not to overcome. He was not confirmed in sin. There is nothing so hardening to the heart, and so blinding to the eyes, and so searing to the conscience as sin. "Those that seek Me early shall find Me." Men who seek late in life, if they truly seek, will find, but it will not be such easy work for them as it is for the young. Young people put off the search, not for ever, but for a time, thinking it can be taken up whenever they please. The will to take up the search is lost by postponement, and the vision of God is made difficult by abandonment to sin. The

pure in heart shall see God. The impure do not.
" Their eyes they have closed, lest they should turn,
and I should heal them." The greatest difficulty
in the way of finding God is not the one made by
the church, or by the times, but by our own sins.
Even that can be overcome ; but God is more
easily, more surely, found by being sought for when
we are young.

II.—JOSIAH WAS RESPONSIVE TO THE WORD.

How plain it seems to have been to him. A
whole book was read to him at a sitting ; and this
same book, entire, was read by him at one service.
There seems to have been no comment. It was
understood as read. There was no school of thought
which said : "This Book can only be understood
by the clergy." No fear was expressed because the
people would accept its contents in their literal
sense. Neither was the intellectual atmosphere
clouded by theories of allegorical or spiritualizing
interpretations. The Book told its own story at
once. If we would read it as these people did, the
impression upon our minds would be very different
from what it is now. Our interest would be captured,
and our obedience would be secured. Then

III.—JOSIAH HAD A TENDER HEART.

He could not read of the judgments which
must befall the people, if they continued in apostasy,

without being moved. He was immediately concerned for Judah and for Israel. He commenced to pray and inquire for himself, and for them. He saw the things that were wrong, and was anxious to remove them. He accepted the corrections of the Word. He did not rebel against them. And out of this tender heart, created by an early search for God, a prolonged reading of the Word, and a ready response to its teaching, the revival was born. This Word that had done him good must be read to others. It must be obeyed. He must make a covenant, and his covenant to obey the law must be an example to his people.

Have we tender hearts? Are we concerned about the indifference and sinfulness of the people? Can we read and know that the way of transgressors is hard, and remain unmoved? Are we content to attend church, and get a few crumbs of comfort for ourselves? Is it nothing to us that the great mass of our fellows are disobedient to God and in great danger? If revival is to come, a tender heart that will be concerned for others must be ours. And if we have not a tender heart we must seek for one. We must be prepared to yield our hearts for considerable periods at a time to the influence of the Word. We must pray for those who are ignorant of God's will. We must be anxious to spread the knowledge of the truth. We must make a covenant to obey the Word; and we must be prepared to

urge others to a like implicit obedience.   If we will
do these things God will use us as He did Josiah,
to produce a religious awakening.

IX.

Under Zerubbabel.

Ezra i., ii., and iii.

BETWEEN the revival under Hezekiah and that under Josiah 104 years elapsed. Eighty-seven years intervened between the latter and a similar event under Zerubbabel. But now in the books of Ezra and Nehemiah we have no less than four recorded in about 90 years. The first one was associated with the first return from Babylon and the laying of the foundations of the new temple, followed 20 years later by an awakening which issued in the completion of the building. More than 50 years passed away before Ezra led a second expedition to Jerusalem ; and then, after an interval of about 13 to 14 years, Nehemiah led a third party. These revivals are all connected with the return from the exile, and each has some special feature giving it a distinct character. The revival in the time of Zerubbabel issued in the building of the temple ; the one with which Ezra's name is associated is connected with the reintroduction of the law ; and Nehemiah's work was largely that of rebuilding the walls of Jerusalem.

After Josiah's reign the kings and the people sank back again into idolatry, with all its accompanying vice and corruption of individual character and national life. The degeneracy of the people was so bad, and the tendency to relapse so habitual, that the defeats, droughts, and commercial depression with which they had been previously continually visited, were not sufficient to bring them to their senses. A time of captivity and exile was required. And so God permitted Nebuchadnezzar to come against the people. This king burnt the temple, destroyed Jerusalem, took Zedekiah prisoner, and carried all who escaped the sword into captivity. Before the exile Jeremiah had prophesied that it would last 70 years ; and towards the end of the period Daniel was moved by this utterance to pray for the Word of the Lord to be accomplished. In two years from his prayer, in the reign of Cyrus the Persian, permission was given for as many as so desired to return to rebuild the temple. Cyrus gave special command concerning the erection of the fallen sanctuary, and urged all who were unable to go and participate in the work to further it with their contributions. The 137th Psalm describes the feelings of the people towards the city which represented their faith. " By the rivers of Babylon, there we sat down ; yea, we wept, when we remembered Zion. We hanged our harps upon the willows in the midst thereof. For there they that carried us away captive required of us a song : and they that wasted us required of us mirth, saying, 'Sing us one of the songs of Zion.' How shall we sing the Lord's song in a strange land ? If I forget thee, O Jerusalem, let my right hand forget her cunning. If I do not remember thee, let my tongue cleave to the roof of my mouth ; if I prefer not Jerusalem above my chief joy.'' In their exile their hearts returned to the God of their fathers. The spiritual return was first ; the geographical expression followed.

A large party, numbering in all nearly 50,000 people, set out under Zerubbabel upon a march of over 800 miles. The same route was covered later, by a much smaller party under Ezra, in four months; so the probabilities are that this expedition occupied from six to eight months. It has been estimated that about one in six of the exiles returned at this time. The object of the pilgrims was religious, not political. The movement was not like the Zionist enterprise of to-day—designed to give the people a national centre and a refuge from oppression—but its purpose was to establish the worship which had been discarded. The numerical strength of the returning Jews, coupled with the large financial support given by those who remained, was evidence of a revival of faith in the people. At Jerusalem the ancient sacrifices were re-instituted, and the foundations of the temple laid amid scenes of great rejoicings.

The first point I wish to emphasise is that *the fruits of revival are permanent.* In our last story we called attention to the repeated back-slidings of the people, and the constant need there was of revival to keep faith alive. These frequent lapses give the appearance that revivals are not only temporary in duration, but also in effect. This, however, is not so. The excitement accompanying them is of a very temporary nature, and there are also some individuals who do not remain true to the vows made in times of religious enthusiasm. But there are some very distinct gains. We are not in a position to gauge the permanent effects of all the revivals in the Bible, but the fruits of the awakenings recorded in the book of Ezra are very marked, and remain with us until this day. After the captivity the Jews never lapsed into idolatry. The backslidings of previous times had always included that. But the discipline of the centuries, and especially the discipline of a prolonged absence in a foreign country, at last told. That Jehovah is the God of the whole earth, that He is One, and that He is spiritual, is now the permanent creed of the children of Abraham. Into formalism, hypocrisy, greed and corruption, the Jew has frequently and for long periods fallen, but the tendency to lapse into the faith of the surrounding nations has been burnt out of him. Ever since the exile he has been true to his faith in the one God. That is a permanent gain.

Another gain is the one we consider in a later story—the re-introduction of the law by Ezra. The law had been given by Moses; but for long periods, sometimes for nearly a century at a time, it was hidden and forgotten. Now it obtains a permanent place. Though its teachings are not always obeyed, it yet occupies a position of authority that makes it the final court of appeal. It was so enthroned in Christ's day that some of His most powerful arguments were based upon the testimony of the law. When the Apostles were called upon to preach a crucified and a risen Christ they made more of the Scripture testimony to these events than they did of the witness of their own eyes. The place that the law obtained in Ezra's time remains to this day. The Christian argument with the Jew is strong because of the common possession of the Old Testament, and because of the nature of its testimony to the claims of Christ.

The great revivals of the Christian era are similar in the permanency of their effects. The Reformation was a time of great enthusiasm. But the emotions stirred by the movement died down. The Protestant churches left their first love, and sank into formalism and indifference. The emancipation, however, of the Bible from the hands of the priests, its translation into the common language of the people, the right of all to read it, and to obey it as they are individually led, are fruits we all enjoy to-day.

The revival of the eighteenth century has left a permanent memorial in the existence of the Methodist churches, churches which numerically are surpassed by no other Free Protestant bodies in the world, and only possibly equalled by one. In his "Popular History of the Free Churches," Silvester Horne devotes a whole chapter to the "Fruits of the Revivals." One of the most notable and permanent," he says, "was an enlarged Christian hymnody." John and Charles Wesley, William Cowper, and John Newton wrote hymns expressive of the theology and experience of the great evangelical awakening. "In the best modern hymn books it is safe to say a very large proportion of hymns represent the faith and aspirations kindled in the Revival period." "A further direction, in which the new moral energy called into activity by the Revival made itself felt, was prison reform. . . . Whitefield and the Wesleys had made a special point of preaching in the prisons. . . But anything like a systematic attack on these dens of filth and disease, and any attempt to improve the character of the prison discipline had yet to be made. The two names that will ever be associated with prison reform in England are John Howard and Elizabeth Fry, both of whom were Nonconformists." "An even more majestic form which the new passion for social reform, born of the revival impulse, took was the agitation for the emancipation of the slaves." "We shall not be wrong if we maintain that the revival of faith and zeal meant among the elder Nonconformists bodies a revival of political ideals." But "there remains to be described the one of all movements due to the Revival which has had the most world-wide effects—the modern missionary movement." These are sentences culled from, and introductory to, pages that describe in detail the movements to which they refer, and trace their connection with the Revival.

Such tremendous results are the justification of revivals. When we speak of praying and working for revival now, we have not in mind the creation of a wave of religious emotion only, but the availing ourselves of the tremendous moral and spiritual forces which God offers to men, and by means of which permanent additions will be made to the religious, social and philanthropic life of the world.

Second, this revival illustrates *how providence co-operates with the good desires and efforts of the people.* "The Lord stirred up the spirit of Cyrus." "Then rose up the chief of the fathers . . . with all them whose spirit God had raised." Providential circumstances were necessary to make it possible for the desires of the people towards Jerusalem to be realized. These circumstances do not obtain when the people are not ripe for their proper use. Under our democratic constitutions, our complaints about our municipal and parliamentary rulers are often silenced by the remark that we get the rulers we deserve. If we have not elected them our apathy has allowed them to creep into their position. But a reading of history makes one feel that it is not only under democratic institutions that we get the rulers we deserve, but under monarchic as well. A good people are generally blessed with a good king, and a bad people cursed with a bad one. God helps those who help themselves. Where there is real moral earnestness amongst the majority, the door will open for any good enterprise upon which the people's heart is set.

The modern missionary movement is a case in point. Before the Church was stirred up to undertake the work of evangelizing the world, the world was practically closed to the gospel. The barriers were not all pagan. Some of them were erected by white men. The East India Company was against missionary enterprise at first. The nineteenth century was remarkable for two things—the growth of the missionary spirit in the churches, and the breaking down of barriers which, in the shape of geographical obstacles, opposition of governments, prejudices of nations, difficulties of language, and deadly climates, stood in the way of the Gospel being taken to all. The few remaining barriers will most certainly be removed with a still further accession of the evangelistic spirit. When the Church is ready to regard the Great Commission of

Christ as her Marching Orders, the Lord will make it His business to make obedience possible. The obstacles which we cannot overcome He removes when we are consecrated enough to seize the opportunities.

Third, this story gives us a *definition of revival.* They "stood up .   .   .   to offer burnt offerings as it is written in the law of Moses .   .   according to the custom, as the duty of every day required." This is a point we have frequently noted—that the work of revival is according to the Word. Revival is obedience ; it is regard for God's law ; it is a return to Him. Those who oppose revivals seize hold of its accidents and condemn them on account of these. It is the excitement and the disorder which they note. The mingling of singing and weeping "so that the people could not discern the noise of the shout of joy from the noise of the weeping of the people," is the point that is denounced. But this is not of the essence of the revival. A revival may produce noise, but it does not consist of it. The real thing is whole-hearted obedience. In Old Testament times it was expressed by the burnt offerings. To-day it goes under the name of consecration.

Then there are people who are friendly to revivals, and who think them productive of much good, but who also fix their attention upon the accidents. Imitation of these they think will give the required effect. They seize hold of the fact that in some places the sermon has been abolished, and that human leadership of a meeting has been nil, and copying these features they have hoped to bring a revival. The result has been a fiasco. When the people of a meeting are possessed by the Spirit of God it is quite possible that His Presence will mean that prayer and testimony and song will be more general; but then these must be the product of His Presence, not the means of bringing Him.

"That the Word of the Lord by the mouth of Jeremiah might be fulfilled, the Lord stirred up the spirit of Cyrus." The Lord has regard for His own Word. The Book may be closed by man, but God has not forgotten its contents, and He is not content for His Word to be unfulfilled. The Book of Daniel shows us that two years before this event Daniel had been stirred by the prophecy of Jeremiah to pray for its fulfilment. The Word of God had created this desire within him. It made him anxious for its promises to be realised. When man responds to God's own desires, and, with Him, is anxious for its programme to be carried out, the day of fulfilment is not far off.

X.

Under Haggai and Zechariah.

Ezra v., vi. ; Haggai i., ii. ; Zech. i., viii.

THE revival which led to the return from Babylon under Zerubbabel, and to the laying of the foundations of the second temple, seems to to have spent itself when opposition to the work took a forceful turn. For nearly 20 years little or nothing was done. The book of Ezra does not describe the condition of things during that time ; but the messages of Haggai throw some light upon the period. The people had listened to the suggestion that the time was not opportune for the Lord's house to be built ; but they had the will, and found the way, to erect elaborate dwellings of their own. Their agricultural and commercial efforts were considerable ; but because their comfort and prosperity were more to them than the Lord's work, the Lord had called for a drought upon all the labour of their hands. They had consequently sown much and brought in little ; their food was not forthcoming in satisfying quantities ; they had earned wages, but only to put them into a bag with

holes.   Haggai and Zechariah were moved by God's
Spirit to call the people to put first things first.   If
they would build God's house, God would bless
them, and no opposition should hinder them.   The
nations would be shaken by Him.   Before Zerubbabel
the mountain should become a plain.   "Not by
might, nor by power, but by My Spirit, saith the
Lord."   Joshua, the high priest, and Zerubbabel,
and the people, responded whole-heartedly to the
words of the prophets.   The work was taken in
hand, and in four years the temple was completed,
amidst demonstrations of great joy.   Notice :

I.—THE CONDITION OF THE PEOPLE PRECEDING REVIVAL.

The book of Haggai, as already referred to,
shows that, on account of the moral decline of the
people, God had visited the land with drought.   The
connection between the moral and material condition of the people is continually emphasized in
the Bible.   Because to-day we are more familiar
with the laws of nature, and can trace more clearly
than our forefathers the causes and effects of natural
events, we are inclined to be satisfied with such
secondary explanations as being all-sufficient.   We
have ceased largely to believe in any moral cause
being connected with drought or plenty.   In the
history of the children of Israel the connection is
certainly insisted on by the Bible writers.   This

connection we either attribute to a theory of life held by the Scripture writers which has since broken down, or, if we accept the Biblical statements as true, we conclude that material blessings and curses were characteristic of the old covenant, but that only spiritual blessings and curses are the features of the new.

Let me remind you that in the Bible this connection is not confined to the Old Testament times, nor to the Israelites who came under the terms of the old covenant. The connection begins with the story of the Fall. The ground is cursed on account of man's sin. The old world was overwhelmed with a flood because the wickedness of man was great. The Cities of the Plain were destroyed because of the immoral condition of the people. The old inhabitants of Canaan were driven out, or exterminated, when their iniquity was full. Egypt, Babylon, and Tyre all fell because of moral failure. Material curses not only befell the Jew in Old Testament days, but were prophesied to be his lot until he returns in life and heart to God, and to Zion's King. The continuance of the Jew, down to our time, in exile and persecution, is an exact fulfilment of the future sketched for him in the Bible, and shows that the material and moral connection still obtains in his case. The material blessedness of the millennial reign of Christ yet to come is, in the Old and New Testaments alike, connected with the spiritual

condition of the inhabitants of the earth.   And the
Apostle Paul, in a passage in which he touches the
heights of spiritual blessedness—namely, in Romans
viii.—tells us that the whole creation is waiting for
the manifestation of the sons of God, and will, after
their revelation, be delivered into the glorious liberty
of the children of God.   The testimony of the Bible
is one for all ages—past, present, and future, on this
point.

South African history is certainly in harmony
with this teaching. Nine-and-a-half years ago, when
the news of the Drummond Castle disaster reached
us, the "Cape Times" summarised the events of
the preceding months as follows :—"The year is
only half-worn as yet, and we have had already the
disastrous Raid, the worst railway accident in South
African records, one of the most horrible dynamite
explosions in the records of the world, the Namaqua-
land famine, rinderpest and scarcity menacing the
whole of South Africa, the Matabele rising and
massacres, and, last, this calamity of the sea, such a
sudden and total loss of a South African liner as has
never yet come into the annals of our great Home-
ward water highway. The news synchronized with
that of the extension of the Matabele trouble in
Mashonaland." Since then we have had the Lang-
berg campaign, the rinderpest over a much wider
area, drought and locusts, and then the terrible war.
The war contained within itself a series of troubles.

When that was over drought and want and commercial depression ensued. For ten years at least disaster has followed disaster as swiftly and as severely as trouble visited the Israelites when they were estranged from God." Before the war ended, in an address which I gave as President of the Baptist Union of South Africa on " South Africa's Greatest Need—a Revival of Religion," I said : " Can we, in view of all the troubles of the past few years, in the face of all the calculations that have been upset, look for a better state of things, even from a material standpoint, without turning to God ? Personally, I confess I have no hope till the Church exercises, on behalf of men, the ministry of intercession committed to it. I do not say I have no hope of the war ceasing till this happens, but that I have no hope of the troubles of South Africa ending till the Church awakes to its duty."

Prophecy is always a risky thing, but I ventured into that field then because I was convinced from a study of the Bible, and confirmed in the view by our history in this country, that our material troubles would not be removed until we had a religious awakening. Our subsequent history gives further confirmatory evidence in this direction ; and I do not hesitate again to prophesy to the effect that, unless we have a revival of religion, our troubles will continue. The commercial depression may lift, but other troubles on a national scale will be ours.

Our hope for material deliverance is in a spiritual awakening.

The missionary literature of this country is full of illustrations of this law of material and spiritual blessings or disasters going together. "Twenty Years in Khama's Country," by the Rev. J. D. Hepburn; and "Garanganze," by Mr. Fred. Arnot, contain some wonderful stories on these lines.

The connection between these two things may be one which we do not understand, but it is possible to accept it as a law, not only on Scriptural grounds, but on scientific as well. Science does not wait to understand before it accepts the testimony of facts. Gravitation is not yet understood, but observation has established beyond the shadow of a doubt that an intimate connection exists between the various heavenly bodies; and reliable calculations and prophecies are based upon the acceptance of this law. Sir Robert Ball, in "The Story of the Heavens," describing the laws of planetary motion, says: "As established by Kepler, these planetary laws were merely the results of observation . . . the laws as they came from Kepler's hands stood out as three independent truths; thoroughly established, but wholly unsupported by any explanations as to why these movements rather than any other movements should be those appropriate for the revolutions of the planets." The later discoveries of Newton regarding gravitation explained these laws which

Kepler discovered, but the laws were accepted in the astronomical world as the result of observation before they were understood. I would plead, on similar lines, for the recognition of the truth of the intimate connection between the material and moral condition of the people.

II.—THE CONDITIONS OF REVIVAL.

This revival was produced by the preaching of Haggai and Zechariah. The contents of their messages we learn from their books, where the conditions of revival are clearly set forth.

The first message was " Arise and build." The people were to be as much concerned about God's house as they were about their own dwellings. They had not found time for God's work, but they had for their own. What place does God's work take in our minds and hearts ? What proportion of our money do we give to it ? How much strength do we devote to it ? Does it occupy our thoughts to any great extent ? Is it given a prominent place in our prayers ? If these questions are answered honestly, we shall soon discover why we have not yet seen a revival.

The plea of tiredness so continually put forward for lack of attendance at worship, and for failure to take any active part in Christian work, is a revelation that the things of God are not prized very highly. We ask God to bend the heavens and

to come down. We want Him to make bare His
arm. His strength must be exercised ; but we ourselves want to take things easily. Unless we are
prepared to labour to the point of weariness, it is
useless to expect God to do any great work amongst
us.

The first condition given by Haggai may be
considered an ecclesiastical one. But moral conditions are as emphatically demanded. "Thus
speaketh the Lord of hosts, saying, Execute true
judgment, and show mercy and compassions every
man to his brother ; and oppress not the widow,
nor the fatherless, the stranger, nor the poor ; and
let none of you imagine evil against his brother in
your heart." "For thus saith the Lord of hosts,
As I thought to punish you, when your fathers pro-
voked Me to wrath, saith the Lord of hosts, and I
repented not : so again have I thought in these
days to do well unto Jerusalem, and to the House
of Judah : fear ye not. These are the things that
ye shall do : Speak ye every man the truth to his
neighbour ; execute the judgment of truth and
peace in your gates ; and let none of you imagine
evil in your hearts against his neighbour ; and love
no false oath : for all these are things that I hate,
saith the Lord." I thought to do well," God says,
but "these are the things which ye shall do." God
distinctly lays down a programme for us to fulfil.
We have not space to dwell upon all the moral

conditions enforced, but there is one which I particularly desire to emphasize, as it is a condition notoriously absent from this country.

"Speak ye every man the truth to his neighbour." "Execute the judgment of truth." "Love no false oath." One of our judges recently had cause to say that perjury was very frequent in South Africa. That describes the state of things in our law courts, where men are put on oath to tell the truth. But it is also true in business. Two persons recently told me they desired to get out of their present positions because they were required by their employers to lie. One of them, a young man, professing to be a Christian, confessed to frequent backsliding. Pressed for the point at which his backsliding commenced, he acknowledged it was whenever he yielded to the pressure to tell a lie." "And if you stick to the truth, what then?" "Well, then," he said, "I am no good; I am not wanted." The responsibility of men who oppress their fellows in this way is tremendous, and I have not the slightest doubt that the heavier share of the burden of the lie will fall on them. But the employees cannot altogether escape from blame. The confession of the young man referred to is one which I have frequently heard. There is an immediate relapse from Christian experience when a lie is told; and a man who knows that untruthfulness means backsliding, and chooses to lie, shows that he holds his living dearer than he does his Christian character. In the majority of cases I believe it to be true that an employer will not dismiss an employee for refusing to tell a lie. Conscientiousness and trustworthiness are invaluable as business assets, and their value is understood even by men who themselves do not possess these characteristics. But even if dismissal be the result of striking against the employer's requirement, Christian men should be prepared to accept it. We need martyrs in business. Men who will risk their living for the truth will assuredly have the martyr's crown. The martyrs were such because they could not say what they did not believe to be true. They too had wives and children dependent upon them, but they were prepared to die sooner than tell a lie. To deny the truth was to forfeit their Christianity. We must learn to regard lying as a thing that God hates. Without a scrupulous regard for the truth we cannot have revival.

XI.

Under Ezra.

EZRA vii.—x.

EIGHTY years have passed since the first return
from Babylon to Jerusalem under Zerubbabel.
Now a second party, numbering in all about 7,000,
are moved to migrate with Ezra. Under his influence
there was first, amongst the exiles in Babylon, a
revival which led to a return to Jerusalem, and then
at Jerusalem itself, amongst the decendants of
Zerubbabel's party, there was an awakening which
culminated in a wholesale putting away of heathen
wives and customs.

In Babylon Ezra gave himself to seek the law
of the Lord, to do it and to teach it. His zeal and
activity made an impression even upon the king,
who gave him liberty to return to Jerusalem to teach
the law there. Like Cyrus, Artaxerxes granted permission to all Jews to go back to Jerusalem ; urged
those who could not or did not want to go, to give
liberally for the service of the house of the Lord ;
and himself, with his princes, contributed handsomely

to the work which the returning exiles were urged to take in hand. Great power was given to Ezra in the appointment of judges and magistrates, and the enforcement of laws, and in administration generally; and commands were issued to the officers of the province to support the cause which Ezra had at heart.

The party set out on the first day of the first month. At Ahava they rested for three days before setting out for the most dangerous portion of the journey. The perils of the expedition seem to have faced Ezra at this point. His party was not composed of trained men. They were not used to fighting, and the route was beset with wild tribes and brigands. The treasure which they carried would be a great attraction to those who lived by violence. Ezra could have asked for an escort, but he was ashamed to do so, because he said, " we had spoken unto the king, saying, ' the hand of our God is upon all them for good that seek Him ; but His power and His wrath is against all them that forsake Him ! ' " So a period of fasting and prayer was prescribed, and the cause submitted to God. The adventures and happenings of the four months' journey, of something like 800 miles, have no more space allotted to them than the brief words : " The hand of our God was upon us, and He delivered us from the hand of the enemy, and of such as lay in wait by the way."

Arriving at Jerusalem, a period of religious services and offerings ensued. The silver and the gold were handed over to the proper authorities; the letters to the King's lieutenants and governors were delivered; and, as directed, these furthered the people and the work of the Lord. Then it was told Ezra that the Jews to whom he had come were not separated from the people of the land, but were doing according to the filthiness of the surrounding nations. This amalgamation of habit and character was due to intermingling in marriage. The statement was a painful revelation to the new leader. Such marriages were contrary to the law of Moses. Ezra was dumbfounded and discouraged. No blessing could be expected with such back-sliding. For a whole day he sat speechless; and those who trembled at God's Word gathered around him in sympathy. In the evening he arose and poured out his soul to God. He asked for nothing. He could only confess the sin and mourn over it, and acknowledge that if God did to them as He had the right to do, they would perish. His grief and prayer had a wonderful effect upon the people; and one of them, Shechaniah by name, expressed their thoughts when he declared that they must deal with the matter and put the strange wives away. But in the work of reformation Ezra must lead. At once the scribe took advantage of the feeling, and bound those present with an oath to do according to Shechaniah's word. Then an assembly was convened ; and, during the days in which the notices were circulating concerning it, Ezra retired to pray and to fast. The assembly met in a great rain, but the people were in earnest. They trembled when their sin was brought home to them. They acknowledged the seriousness of it, and resolved to deal with it in a thorough manner ; but they pleaded for time. It was not a matter which could be attended to in a few hours, or even days. Wives and children could not be summarily dismissed. They had rights and were entitled to consideration. Courts must sit to judge the various matters that demanded attention. The decision was taken then and there to end the prevailing state of things, but time was allowed for affairs to be settled as humanely and justly as possible. This occupied two months, but the work was done as decided.

I.—EZRA AND THE LAW.

The work of revival began in Ezra. He " had prepared his heart to seek the law of the Lord, and to do it, and to teach in Israel statutes and judgments." This means he made up his mind, and determined to know the law of the Lord. This was to be his particular study. He is portrayed as " a ready scribe in the law of Moses," "a scribe of the words of the Commandments of the Lord, and of His statutes to Israel." He was a copyist of the law. To seek the law means he determined upon making an accurate copy. This meant much research, and labour ; but if he were to do and teach it he must be prepared for this.

We do not have to make our own copies to-day; they are made for us. But we should see to it that we each get a good and a readable one. It is the burden of many sincere souls that their Bibles yield them neither pleasure nor profit. The Scriptures are tiring to many, because they attempt to read them under conditions under which they would not think of doing their ordinary reading. There is no book that people attempt to read in such small type as they do the Bible. They are handicapped for pleasure at the start. Reading is necessarily irksome under such conditions. Pocket Bibles have their use, but a person who only possesses one of these will never be a Bible reader. It is a strain to continue reading more than a few verses at the time. The same is true of the ordinary Teacher's Bible. Maps, helps, references, etc., are all packed within a small compass, and the text of the Scriptures is again painfully small. Whatever other Bibles may be added, the first one should be chosen, not for its portableness, its helps, or wide margins for notes, but for its good print, and so for comfortable and easy reading.

The next thing is to learn to obey the Word. Jesus puts great emphasis upon the doing of His will. "Not every one that saith unto Me, Lord, Lord, shall enter into the kingdom of heaven ; but he that doeth the will of My Father which is in heaven." Those who hear and do are likened unto the man building his house upon the rock ; but those who hear only are compared to the man who builds his house upon the sand. "If ye continue in My words, then are ye My disciples indeed." "He that rejecteth Me, and receiveth not My words, hath one that judgeth him : the word that I have spoken, the same shall judge him in the last day." Our attitude to the words of Jesus determines our attitude to Jesus Himself. All the titles which we are prepared to grant to Him count for nothing if we do not His will as revealed in His utterances.

Having learnt the law and practised it, Ezra taught it. He did not teach before he had learnt to do. But he found obedience possible, and when he had demonstrated this, he felt free to teach. We cannot urge to an obedience higher than the one we find practicable for ourselves. The measure of our teaching is set by our doing.

II.—Ezra and his God.

Ezra knew so much about God, talked so often about Him, and did His will so constantly, that he and God became identified, and the names of God and Ezra were coupled together. Up to a point the narrative in the book of Ezra is written in the third person. The author of this portion speaks of the good hand of " his God " being upon him. Then Artaxerxes, addressing Ezra, says, " thy God." Ezra himself says, " my God." Ezra confessed to a personal relationship existing between himself and God ; and the testimony of those writing to him, and of him, in the second and the third persons, is evidence that his life made good this claim.

Ezra became identified with God, because God and His law were the prevailing topics with him. Just note what a knowledge of God the heathen king obtained through Ezra's testimony. Artaxerxes speaks of " the God of heaven," "the God of Israel," "thy God." He knows the Lord has a house, that this is at Jerusalem, that He has given a law, and that this law is embodied in a book which is in Ezra's hands. The law of God is a law to do, and one capable of being taught and understood. There is a service of God's house ; and what the requirements of this service are in men, money, furniture and sacrifices, is known to the king.

And this testimony which Ezra gave about God was one that committed him to a faithful and consistent life. There were things which he was prevented from doing, because they would appear inconsistent with it. He was ashamed, he tells us, to ask for an escort, because of the witness he had given to the king about the loving care of his God. Here is the value of testimony. It not only informs others about God, but it helps to keep us straight. It makes a standard by which we are bound to endeavour to live. And when we tremble as Ezra did before the difficulties of consistency, we, like him, are compelled, in our weakness, to pray for strength. Testimony about our God compels consistency, and trust, and prayer.

III.—Ezra and the Hand of the Lord.

One of Ezra's characteristic expressions is "the hand of the Lord." "The king granted him all his request, according to the hand of the Lord his God upon him." "He came to Jerusalem according to the good hand of his God upon him." "I was strengthened as the hand of the Lord my God was upon me." "By the good hand of our God upon us they brought us a man of understanding." "The hand of our God was upon us, and He delivered us from the hand of the enemy."

For the hand of the Lord to be upon us means that we are under its direction. It guides; and we are obedient to its leadings. It protects, and none can pluck us out of His hand. It also provides. It brings help to us as required. And it strengthens us for work. It gives us confidence that when guided by Him we shall not fail.

IV.—Ezra and the People's Sin.

The transgression of the people was a burden

to Ezra. It was a personal sorrow. It took the heart out of him, and robbed him of his appetite. He mourned and confessed as if he himself had transgressed. The awfulness of it came home to him. He knew there could be no prosperity whilst these unhallowed and unauthorized unions lasted. They had not merely committed a mistake ; they had sinned and had forfeited God's favour. They had no claim upon Him. Only by an act of marvellous clemency on God's part could the past be blotted out.

It was this sense of sin which gave to Ezra his power. His consciousness of sin created a similar one in the people. They trembled on account of their transgression. For years they had lived in this condition, without a qualm of conscience. But now God's law, working in a heart to whom that law was a power, quickened their consciences, and they became aware of the awfulness of their condition.

We need to-day a greater sense of sin. There will be no serious attempt to be separated from it all the time we think of it as weakness and as being excusable. Whilst we shut our eyes to the great penalties attached to sin, and whilst we regard the pardon of God as a right to which we are entitled, but expressive of no particular grace on His part, we shall not make a life and death struggle with it. The people around us are light-hearted in the life which they are living of alienation from God. Their condition does not trouble them. The people around Ezra were in a similar mood until he discovered to them by God's law, and his own God-given horror and concern, the heinousness of their transgression. We must allow God's Word to reveal to us the state of the people. God's estimate of sin, and not man's, must rule in our hearts. The measure of our appreciation of the Cross of Christ, which tells us of the tremendous sacrifice needed by God to end this matter, will be the measure of our power to turn the people from their sins.

XII

Under Nehemiah.

THIS is the longest of all the revival stories in the Bible ; and it forms a part of that series which originated in Babylon. Making inquiries concerning Jerusalem, and the Jews resident there, Nehemiah learnt that the people were in great affliction and reproach, and that the walls of the city were broken down, and the gates thereof burnt with fire. This news aroused a deep concern in his heart, so much so that for days he sat down and wept, and mourned, and fasted and prayed. Day and night he presented his petition before God. He confessed the sins of the people, and pleaded the promises given through Moses, and then asked that God would prosper him and grant him mercy in the sight of the King. He was the King's cupbearer, and, as such, was either a favourite or in a position where it was possible to become one. Four months seemed to have passed before the desired opportunity to speak to the King came to him. But by that time plans had formed in his mind and he had a programme ready. It was

the duty of all who appeared before the King to have
a cheerful countenance, and until now Nehemiah
had not been sad in his presence. But his sorrow was
so great that he was unable to disguise it. Artaxerxes
made sympathetic inquiries concerning his trouble ;
and Nehemiah, feeling the critical moment had come,
was sore afraid, but in response to an invitation to
make known his requests. He "prayed to the God
of heaven, and said unto the King, 'If it please the
King, and if thy servant have found favour in thy
sight, that thou wouldest send me unto Judah, unto
the city of my fathers' sepulchres, that I may build
it.' " The permission was granted, an escort
provided ; and letters, authorising him to proceed
with the work, were given to be presented to all the
officials concerned.

Arriving at Jerusalem, Nehemiah made a mid-
night inspection of the fallen walls before he
revealed his intentions to anyone. Then calling
together the rulers he said : " Ye see the distress
that we are in, how Jerusalem lieth waste, and the
gates thereof are burned with fire : come, and let us
build up the wall of Jerusalem, that we be no more
a reproach." His words had a stimulating effect,
and the decision was made to rise and build. The
work was divided out into sections and all were
stirred to take a part. In seven weeks the walls were
completed. There was much opposition from the
enemies of the Jews. This took various forms :

scoffing, a threatened attack, an invitation to a conference, and a probable trap, an open letter containing a false accusation, and an attempt to lure Nehemiah into an act of cowardice so as to undermine his authority. But these efforts were successfully met with prayer, watchfulness, wisdom, courage and activity.

Whilst this work was in progress, a great cry arose amongst the poorer Jews against the oppressions and exactions of their richer brethren. In order to buy food in time of drought, and also to meet the excessive taxes exacted by various governors for themselves and the King, many had been compelled to mortgage their houses, lands and vineyards. A ruinous rate of interest had been charged. One per cent per month, equal to 12 per cent. per annum, had brought some of them to the position of having to sell their sons and daughters and themselves into bondage, and this to their own brethren. Nehemiah was very angry when these things were made known to him. He rebuked the nobles strongly for their action, and pointed out the reproach it brought upon God's cause. He urged them to restore everything they had obtained in this way, property, goods and money, and to grant liberty to those who had sold themselves. The fact that the nobles responded to this appeal at once is proof of the deep character of the revival that was taking place. With such restoration, and with a purpose to discontinue such practices, none of them could ever be very rich.

When the walls were finished, the people requested that Ezra should bring the book of the law and read to them. From the morning to mid-day they stood whilst Ezra, upon a pulpit of wood, read the word, " and gave the sense and caused them to understand the reading." The first effect was a painful one. It discovered their sins to them, and they mourned and wept. It was with difficulty they were quieted and told that the time was one for rejoicing and feasting. God had visited them ; His law had been given ; and they should " make great mirth, because they had understood the words that were declared unto them." The next day the reading was resumed. This time an omission was revealed to them. The Feasts of Tabernacles had been frequently observed, but one item had not received attention. They had not erected the booths which were to remind them of the condition of their wilderness life, and which were to arouse gratitude as these conditions were contrasted with the more permanent character of their town and city dwellings. This matter having been rectified, they gathered again for seven days. For three hours each day they listened to the Word ; and a similar period was spent in confession and worship. The cumulative effect of the reading of the law was that a covenant was made to keep the commandments of the Lord. In this covenant special mention was made against foreign marriages, Sabbath labour and trade, and the exaction of interest. Ordinances were also made concerning the support of the temple worship. An annual payment in cash was to be made by each; and a tithe of the produce of the land and of the fruit of the cattle was to be rendered regularly. They said: " We will not forsake the house of our God."

This covenant was made whilst they were still in great temporal distress. " Behold," they said, " we are servants this day, and for the land that thou gavest unto our fathers to eat the fruit thereof and the good thereof, behold we are servants in it; and it yieldeth much increase unto the Kings whom thou hast set over us because of our sins : also they have dominion over our bodies, and over our cattle, at their pleasure, and we are in great distress. And because of all this we make a sure covenant."

Their consciences were aroused concerning the injustices of which they had been guilty one towards another. These they felt compelled to put right. But their consciences were also sensitive to the injustices that others were doing to them. It was not in their power to remove these, so they humbly submitted to them, and accepted them as the desert and harvest of their sins. Their condition was one which would have embittered many and turned them against God. But these people give it as one of the reasons why they made a covenant. Their acceptance of their lot is one of the evidences of the revival of faith.

This revival was one of the most extensive recorded in the Scriptures. It took the form of a patriotic interest in their city, as seen in the building of the walls; the creation of a new spirit of brotherhood as they engaged in a common task, which issued in the rectifying of many wrong relationships; a new interest in the law; a resolution to be obedient to its teachings; and a determination to maintain public worship and the services in God's house. The awakening was civic, social, moral, ecclesiastical and spiritual. It affected heart and mind and conduct. It touched church life, home life, business life and civic life. The revivals of the Bible are eminently practical.

Let me call your attention to some of the active causes of this awakening. And first, we must mention *Nehemiah's concern for the people.* Both their temporal and spiritual condition stirred his soul. Their poverty and persecution cast him down, and their iniquities made him angry. Each called for thought and action and prayer. The compassion of Jesus was of this double order. He would not send the multitudes hungry away lest they should faint on the road. Moved with compassion He healed the sick. But their shepherdless condition equally affected Him. Beholding the city He wept over it, and said : " How often would I have gathered thy children together even as a hen gathereth her chickens under her wings, and ye would not." In all healthy spiritual life these two things must go together. George Muller was great at prayer, but equally great in his care for the orphans. C. H. Spurgeon preached to the multitudes; but he also built almshouses and orphanages. General Booth is the evangelist of the lapsed masses; but also one who organizes relief and rescue works on a large scale. True Christianity is concerned for the people in this world as well as the next. And those who shew the deepest concern for the state of the soul are generally those who do most for the people in this present life. The realization of the value of the soul has increased the estimate of the body that enshrines it. We must care for the whole of man.

The concern of Nehemiah affected him in public and in private. In private he wept and fasted and prayed. In public his countenance was sad, not always so, but until a door opened to deal with his distress. The concern which will result in blessing for the people is one that continues with us after our worship has ceased, and after we have got from under the influences of stirring speech, and song, and that remains with us during the working hours. When Nehemiah was serving the King the thought of his people's condition affected him. The spiritual state of the people is no real burden to us if we only consider it when we are brought face to face with it in church. The burden of a sinful world is ever present to those whom God uses to bring the people back to Himself.

Second, *Nehemiah's concern for the people moved him to prayer.* His prayers were not perfunctory, or inspired by a mere sense of duty, but they were expressive of deep feeling. He tells us he prayed day and night. The much speaking which Christ condemns is the needless repetition of phrases such as, "O Baal, hear us; O Baal, hear us." But the constant expression of desires that are always with us, and which find relief in utterance, is the praying without ceasing to which we are urged. The efficacy of prayer depends not upon the phraseology but upon the intensity, as well as the rightness, of the desires of the heart. Prayers that are not inspired by strong feeling will be resultless.

Nehemiah prayed over everything. When he was concerned about his brethren he brought their condition before God. When he was confronted with the need of the King's consent to his expedition, and the fact that this same King had given orders on a previous occasion for the building of the wall to cease, he prayed that he might find favour in his sight. When his heart trembled in the presence of the King, and he feared to make his request, he prayed unto the God of heaven. When the sneers of Sanballat and Tobiah hurt him, he found relief in prayer. When he and his men were in danger, and when false reports were circulated concerning him, he brought these things before God.

This habit of prayer made it natural for him to pray anywhere. When alone he could pour out his heart to God. But when in the presence of the King, and in the act of serving him, and suddenly confronted with a serious question, he could sandwich a prayer between the King's question and his own answer. The prayer was in his heart unheard by the King. " I prayed to the God of heaven, and I said unto the King."

But this spiritually-minded man who prayed over everything, and everywhere, to whom prayer was almost as natural as breathing, is one of the most practical, level-headed men that ever lived. Some of God's answers to his prayers came along the line of his own thinking. After praying he would plan, and then he would act. By the time the King had recognized his sorrow he had planned to go to Jerusalem, to obtain the King's consent to the project, to have letters to speed him on his way and to authorize him to get timber for the work of restoration. When he arrived at Jerusalem he surveyed the situation before he outlined the work to the rulers. He consulted with himself before he rebuked the nobles concerning their exactions. His plan of defence against attack was a masterly one. Cromwell has been credited with the phrase, "Trust in God and keep your powder dry." But the idea belongs to Nehemiah, " Nevertheless we made our prayer unto God, and set a watch against them day and night."

Nehemiah's concern, prayer, thought, activity and testimony, were the means God used to awaken the conscience of the people and to bring them back to their allegiance to the Lord.

XIII.

Under John the Baptist.

MATT. iii. ; MARK i. ; LUKE iii. ; JOHN i. and iii.

THE preaching of John the Baptist produced the first revival recorded in the New Testament. His meetings were held in the open air. How he first reached the people we do not know. The record tells of the people coming to him rather than of him going to them. The crowds were so tremendous that the evangelist says, "Then went out to him Jerusalem, and all Judæa, and all the region round about Jordan." Every village and hamlet in the district had representatives at his services. The results were no less remarkable than the crowds. The overwhelming majority of his congregations were converted, for Mark says, "They were all baptized of him in the river Jordan, confessing their sins." The unbaptized were the exceptions, and these exceptions were made up of Pharisees and Sadducees. Another striking feature of John's work was that whilst his success at first was judged by the large numbers who flocked to him, it was afterwards measured by the diminution of his congregations. His work was to prepare men to receive Christ; and when Jesus came on the scenes the people left John to listen to him. And that Jesus took a greater place in their affections than the Baptist was a testimony to the faithfulness of the forerunner's ministry. Probably no other man's success has ever been measured by his power to detach people from himself to another.

The revival under John was essentially a preaching one, and the preaching was of repentance. "Repent ye, for the kingdom of heaven is at hand," is the summary which Matthew gives of his message. Mark says: "John did preach the baptism of repentance for the remission of sins." "Bring forth fruits meet for repentance," is an exhortation recorded by Matthew and Luke. The repentance preached was a preparation for the reception of the coming king, and for a place in the coming kingdom. These two topics preached with vigour, earnestness, sincerity, and plainness of speech were the causes of the revival which ensued. With these I therefore propose to deal under the one heading of Repentance.

I.—THE PLACE OF REPENTANCE IN EVANGELISTIC PREACHING.

The word repent is the first one used by John. It occupies the same position in the ministry of Jesus. "Jesus began to preach and to say, 'Repent for the kingdom of heaven is at hand.'" The first word of command spoken at Pentecost was "Repent," which Peter gave in response to the question of the people,— "Men and brethren, what shall we do?" Paul declared that "God now commandeth all men everywhere to repent"; and summing up his ministry at Ephesus he said: "I have taught you publicly, and from house to house, testifying both to the Jews, and also to the Greeks, repentance toward God, and faith toward our Lord Jesus Christ."

Jesus declared one purpose of His coming was "to call sinners to repentance"; also that "it behoved Christ to suffer, and to rise again from the dead the third day, and that repentance and remission of sins should be preached." Peter declared that Jesus had been raised "to give repentance and remission of sins unto Israel." So we have it stated that Jesus came, suffered, and rose from the dead, all to make repentance possible to men.

Then the apostles were especially instructed on this one point. Their training was directed to the effectual preaching of repentance. To them were committed the keys of the kingdom of heaven. Jesus speaks of the "key of knowledge." They had the knowledge which, imparted to the people, opened the kingdom of heaven to them. One of the keys was repentance. They also had power to remit and to retain sins; and Jesus promised to ratify in heaven what in His name they did on earth. They had not power in His name to do anything they liked; but they had power to do as He instructed them; and He gave them authority to declare to men the terms on which their sins would be remitted. Repentance was in these terms. That knowledge has now been committed to writing, and can be used by us all. On the authority of God's Word we can tell men that if they repent and turn to Jesus their sins will be blotted out; and wherever men accept that testimony and act accordingly they will find Jesus in heaven ratifying it. He still stands by His word, and gives His Holy Spirit to bear witness with the spirits of those who obey Him.

The primary position taken by repentance in the preaching of John the Baptist, Jesus, and the Apostles; its declared relationship to the Incarnation, Death, and Resurrection of Christ; its place in the Great Commission as a duty to be preached to all nations; and its connection with the remission of sins and admission to the kingdom of heaven, all require that it should be more pressed in the preaching of the day than is usually the case. Unless repentance is given an equal prominence to that which it had when the Christian Church was started, the preaching of to-day will not issue in revival.

II.—THE CHARACTER OF THE REPENTANCE REQUIRED.

This we learn from the word itself. It means

" a change of mind." A man says he will not do a certain thing. He eventually does it, and explains that he changed his mind. A change of mind affects action.

In John's instructions he detailed how repentance was to be expressed. " Fruits of repentance " was his phrase. Men were to share their plenty with the destitute ; the taxgatherers were to be honest, and only to exact what was due ; and the soldiers were to do violence to no man, neither to accuse any falsely, and were to be content with their wages.

A consideration of the position of the people to whom Peter gave the command to repent on the day of Pentecost will help to an understanding of the subject. These men had joined in the cry, "We have no king but Cæsar." Concerning Christ they had said, " We will not have this man to reign over us." Now they discover that God had made Him both Lord and Christ. In view of the fact that they have rejected Him and that He is now in a position of power, they feel their position to be a very serious one, and they say, "What shall we do ? " The reply, " Repent, and be baptized every one of you in the name of Jesus Christ for the remission of sins, and ye shall receive the gift of the Holy Ghost," practically meant that they must change their minds about Christ. They must reconsider their position towards Him. Instead of rejecting Him they must accept

Him. And this is the message we have to urge upon men to-day. "We have turned every one to his own way." "The carnal mind is enmity against God ; for it is not subject to the law of God." We have said in our hearts, "No God ; we do not want one. Religion is restraint. Let us cast its cords from us." We have to change our minds about whose will shall govern us, our own or Christ's. The question is, whether we shall be our own lords or whether Jesus shall be King. Repentance, admitting to the kingdom of heaven, is a change of mind about Christ.

Such repentance may have much or little emotional sorrow about it. It is not the degree of sorrow, or emotion, that gives it its virtue, neither is it the length of the sorrow. There is no necessity for men who hear the command to spend nights in tears, or to undergo any prolonged agony, before they come into the light. Experiences of this kind vary according to temperament, scriptural knowledge, or the tenacity with which one holds on to some favourite sin. When the command comes to a man clearly, it is possible for him to obey it at once. Any man who can clearly define his position towards Jesus as follows : "I accept Jesus as my God and Saviour, and will endeavour to learn His will, and will at all times do it, even though my will be different from what I can see His to be," has repented, and, though he has not passed through the agony of Luther or of Bunyan, can, on the authority of God's Word, rejoice in the knowledge that his sins are pardoned, and that he is accepted as a child of God.

III.—THE MOTIVES FOR REPENTANCE.

John gave three reasons why men should repent.

1. *For the kingdom of heaven is at hand.* The Jewish ideas of the kingdom were material. It has frequently been said that Jesus replaced this with the idea of a spiritual kingdom. But He did nothing of the kind. The material kingdom for which the Jew was looking is still to come. The mistake made was not in thinking of it as material, but in thinking only of the material, and having no thought of spiritual fitness for it. Because they were the children of Abraham the Jews thought they would inherit it. John corrected this idea, and showed them they could not enter it unless there was a change of character brought about by repentance. Jesus said many would come from the East and from the West and would sit down in the kingdom of heaven with Abraham, Isaac, and Jacob, whilst many of their physical descendants would be cast out. Jesus insisted upon humility, meekness, love of peace and righteousness, and other spiritual qualities, as being required for the kingdom. The spiritual state was to come first. The promise of inheriting the earth still remained, but it would be fulfilled to the meek, not to the Jew as such.

After the Resurrection the apostles looked for the establishment of the temporal kingdom. They said : " Lord, wilt Thou at this time restore again the kingdom to Israel ? " Jesus did not at this point reply, " Have I been so long time with you, and yet hast thou not understood Me ? " These men were to preach the gospel of the kingdom. For this they had been trained. They were within a few days of commencing their ministry. If they were wrong on this point they must be corrected. But they were not wrong. Jesus simply said : " It is not for you to know the times or the seasons, which the Father hath put in His own power. But ye shall receive power after that the Holy Ghost is come upon you ; and ye shall be witnesses unto Me both in Jerusalem, and in all Judæa, and in Samaria, and unto the uttermost part of the earth." He gave them a work to do. That was the thing they were to trouble about. The time of the setting up of the kingdom was in the Father's hands. Let them fulfil their programme first, and God's part would soon be accomplished. In harmony with this is Peter's declaration after Pentecost : " Repent ye therefore, and turn again, that your sins may be blotted out, that so there may come seasons of refreshing from the presence of the Lord ; and that He may send the Christ who hath been appointed for you, even Jesus ; whom the heaven must receive until the times of restoration of all things." Repentance is a pre-requisite to the kingdom. The kingdom has two forms : a present spiritual one, and a future material one. Repentance is necessary for entrance into that state where Jesus rules now ; and membership of the spiritual kingdom is the condition of having a place in the kingdom when realised materially in the future.

2. *For the remission of sins.* It is God who forgives sins. It is the blood of Jesus that cleanses us from sin. As the Lamb of God, Jesus bears away the sin of the world. The Lord hath laid on Him the iniquity of us all. Without the shedding of blood there is no remission. Forgiveness of sins is a tremendous business. It is the most costly of all the things undertaken by God. And being so great, man can do nothing to win it. The whole work must be undertaken by God. But forgiveness having been made possible, it comes to man with a command attached. Man has something to do in order to receive it. He has to repent. He is commanded to repent. The condition is one which he can fulfil. Any man who wills to turn can do so. And if a man does not repent he cannot be forgiven. "Except ye repent, ye shall all likewise perish."

3. *The Wrath to Come.* John urged men to flee from the wrath to come. That wrath was the wrath of God executed by Jesus. John expressed it under the figure of fire. The fire may not be literal ;

but whatever it is, it will not be less terrible than the figure. Paul, too, uses the coming judgment as a reason why men should repent : " God commandeth all men everywhere to repent ; because He hath appointed a day, in the which He shall judge the world in righteousness by that Man Whom He hath ordained ; whereof He hath given assurance unto all men, in that He hath raised Him from the dead." Men think of judgment as vindictive, hard, and unfair. Paul tells us " God will judge the world in righteousness." There will be perfect justice. And the Judge is " that Man whom He hath ordained." Jesus has been tempted in all points as we are. In human nature He has met the enemy. He knows the strength and cruelty of his assaults. The Judge being Jesus we may rest assured that everything that can be said on man's behalf will be said. For Jesus is not only Judge, He is Advocate too. When He was upon the Cross He could find something to say for His murderers. The Judge of all mankind is by no means devoid of tenderness. The terrible thing is not that He will be the Judge, but that men will persist in sin till even Jesus, who speaks for men when no one else can say a word, will be compelled to condemn. There is coming a time when sin has to be finished, and if men remain sinners until then their case will be hopeless.

XIV.

Pentecost.

The revival at Jerusalem on the day of Pentecost is the greatest of all time. In every respect it occupies the first place. No revival was ever so sudden, none so tremendous in its immediate effects, and none so lasting in its results. One hundred and twenty disciples of the Lord Jesus were suddenly baptized in the Holy Spirit. Their characters were wonderfully enriched. New gifts of speech, insight, and argument were conferred upon them. A great accession of zeal, and love, and devotion was added to their motive powers. Within a few hours 3,000 men and women were converted. The Christian Church was constituted. Every day conversions took place; sometimes scores, hundreds, and even thousands, were added to the ranks of the disciples. The work continued for years in Jerusalem itself. It was not the event of a season. It also spread abroad. The revival created missionaries, who went out in all directions. Revivals in other centres followed. Every city of any considerable importance in the Roman Empire felt the influence of the movement during the next few years. This revival made the Apostles, it created the Church, it caused its expansion, it inspired the Epistles, it spread Christianity throughout the whole known earth. The influence of it has reached to our own time. The Church has had a fluctuating history; it has seen many ups and downs, but the power of Pentecost has never been completely lost. A power was sent into the world at that time which has never left it. All the good in the history of the Church is due to the presence of the Holy Spirit. To tell the story fully is to give the whole history of Christian enterprise. The revival that issued in the translation and circulation of the Bible, the Reformation, the Evangelical Revival, the Revival of Missions, the 1859 Revival, the Welsh Revival, are all phases of this one great Pentecostal blessing. Pentecost contained all these in germ; and as Pentecost is studied and understood it tends to repeat itself.

Just as the full result of Pentecost cannot be told, so neither can its causes. To account for it one must deal with the Incarnation, the Death, the Resurrection, the Ascension, and the Heavenly Ministry of Jesus; also with the relationship existing between God the Father, God the Son, and God the Holy Ghost; also the relationship of God to man and of Christ to man. "This Jesus hath God raised up . . . Therefore, being by the right hand of God exalted, and having received of the Father the promise of the Holy Ghost, He hath shed forth this, which ye now see and hear."

Upon all the features of Pentecost one cannot dwell. The outstanding event is, however, the gift of the Holy Spirit, and that is the point which we will emphasize.

I.—THE GIFT OF THE SPIRIT WAS A FULFILMENT OF THE WORD.

The serious questioning of some, and the scoffing of others, about the ecstasies of the disciples, were answered by Peter in these words : " This is that which was spoken by the prophet Joel." God had remembered His Word. Though spoken hundreds of years earlier, the promise still held good. When hundreds of years elapse between promise and fulfilment men begin to question the promise. " Where is the promise of His coming ? " they say. But no lapse of time makes God forget or nullify His promises. Jesus Himself had reiterated the promise of the Spirit. And as Jesus led His disciples through the Word and pointed out what God had undertaken to do for them, their faith and expectancy became great.

Every revival is a fulfilment of the Word. And every revival comes through some men laying hold of the promises and believing in them. We must allow the Word to create within us a spirit of expectancy. If our experiences are below the promises

of God we must question the former, not the latter.
Our interpretation of God's Word must not be
governed by our low condition ; but our experiences
must be corrected by and levelled up to the Word.
The promise of the Spirit remains. Centuries have
not worn it out. It meets our need. It is just what
we require. It also echoes God's heart. It is not
merely to fulfil His Word, and to prove that He is
faithful, that He is willing still to give the Holy
Spirit, but it is the desire of His heart. He wants
to bless men with His Spirit.

As a fulfilment of the Word the gift of the
Spirit answers doubt. Those who had doubted
Christ were convinced at Pentecost. The men who,
believing Him to be a fraud, had crucified Him,
now accepted Him as Lord. And this without
seeing the empty tomb, or first searching in vain for
His body. There was a testimony given direct to
their consciences and hearts that was convincing.
All kinds of intellectual difficulties vanish before the
convincing presence of the Holy Ghost. The
presence of the Holy Spirit in transformed lives
answers doubt as nothing else can. The greatest
argument for the truth of God's Word is a great
work of the Spirit. Nothing has such evidential
value as this.

II.—THE GIFT OF THE HOLY SPIRIT GIVES
THE POWER OF CONTINUANCE.

In the Old Testament the revivals were of very

short duration. Some of them only lasted a few weeks. Zeal for God on the part of the many seldom lasted more than a year or two. The prophet himself seemed to possess the power to continue ; and by extraordinary exertions and zeal he was able to whip the people temporarily to a quickened pace. But when he was out of the way they backslid. When the Lord raised up a judge the people served the Lord all the days of the judge, but when he died they turned again to idols. And this faithfulness of the people of God, that was dependent upon the faithfulness of the judge, was a characteristic of the times of the prophets as well.

But now we enter upon a new era. " Behold the days come, saith God, when I will make a new covenant with the house of Judah : not according to the covenant that I made with their fathers in the day when I took them by the hand to lead them out of the land of Egypt ; because they continued not in my covenant." The feature of non-continuance is eliminated by the gift of the Spirit. It is necessary for men to endure to the end in order to be saved ; and the gift of endurance is supplied by Christ. Of the men and women who accepted God's offer of His Spirit on the day of Pentecost, we read : " And they continued steadfastly." " Many wonders and signs were done by the Apostles," but the multitudes "continued steadfastly with one accord." When the people were driven from Jerusalem by persecution, "they that were scattered abroad went about preaching the Word." The apostles remained at Jerusalem. The people were not dependent upon them for their zeal; they had the power of continuance within them of God. When the Ethiopian eunuch continued his journey toward the south—after Philip the evangelist, the man who led him into the light, had left him—he went on his way rejoicing. Though without Christian fellowship he was all right, for he had learnt the closer fellowship which in the Spirit is possible with the Father and the Son.

When people are urged to declare themselves on the Lord's side they often reply that they would, only they fear they would not be able to hold out. They forget that continuance in the Christian life is not dependent upon natural ability to persevere, but that it is a distinct Christian grace conferred upon the one who truly surrenders to Jesus.

III.—THE GIFT OF THE SPIRIT CHANGES AND SAVES MEN.

A great change was wrought in the Apostles by the gift of the Spirit. They were already comparatively good men. Under the teaching and influence of Christ for three years a great improvement in their characters had taken place. But they were still weak. Though sincerely desirous of being true to Jesus, Peter had found the laugh and scoff of a servant girl too much for his loyalty. He could not confess his Lord before the soldiers gathered around the fire at night. But now he is ready to face thousands of scoffing, hostile men. He can brave the scholars of the Sanhedrim. He can receive 39 stripes from a cruel tearing scourge, and depart from his beating rejoicing that he was counted worthy to suffer dishonour for the Name ; and saying, to those who command him to preach no more, that he must obey God rather than men.

We have men who tell us that they can live good lives without being Christians. We do not need to deny their statement. But we reply that the best of men are wonderfully improved by the gift of God's Spirit. If without Him some are as good as they claim to be, what possibilities are before them by yielding to the absolute rule of Christ. When the judgment sits we shall find that what we might have been will be taken into account quite as much as what we are.

But the gift of the Spirit not only changes men ; it saves them. Peter said : " Save yourselves from this crooked generation." Science has unfolded to us in these modern times the law of environment. It is a great law. But it is neither new, nor newly discovered. In Peter's day men thought they must be shaped by their surroundings ; and they pleaded as earnestly as men do now that the age and companionship were against them being different from what they were. Environment is too strong a law for the majority of men to stand against by themselves ; but God knows our frame, He remembers that we are dust. The promise of the Spirit is His recognition of our need. When He comes, it is then true that " greater is He that is in you than He that is in the world." The Spirit of God is stronger than the spirit of the age ; and by His power a man can be saved from his generation and be made different from the ordinary run of men.

IV.—THE GIFT OF THE SPIRIT IS A DIVINE GIFT.

Such a tremendous gift may suggest to us the need of a superhuman power to reach after Him or to receive Him. It is well to remember we are talking of a gift, not of a Power or a Person acquired, overtaken, or seized. And this gift is a Divine one. It is Divine power which is put forth in the importation of the Holy Spirit. We have not to fix our faith upon our capacity for receiving, but upon God's power to give.

Such a great blessing also suggests to us a measure of worthiness. So we must add to our thought of Divine power that of Divine grace. It might be said that the disciples by their training and power had been made worthy of His coming. But that cannot be said of the multitudes. The crowds consisted of Christ's enemies. They were charged by Peter with the responsibility of crucifying Him. And yet to these Peter said, " The promise is to you, and to your children, and to all that are afar off, even to as many as the Lord our God shall call." Again let us emphasize that the Holy Spirit is a gift. He is not a reward. Divine power and Divine grace impart. And the condition of acceptance is a complete surrender to the Lordship of Christ.

XV.

In Samaria.

ACTS viii., 1-25.

SAMARIA was the first place outside of Jerusalem to feel the effect of Pentecost. But though Pentecost was such a tremendous revival it was a few years before its influence spread beyond the City. The church consisted of thousands of people and was being added to daily, and yet no organized effort was made to give the Gospel message to those in other parts. The persecution that broke out upon the death of Stephen thrust the people forth; and "they that were scattered abroad went about preaching the word." Philip went to the city of Samaria. His preaching, and his works of healing, called forth faith from the multitudes. The people in large numbers believed, and were baptized. When the news reached Jerusalem the Apostles sent Peter and John down; and the Holy Spirit was given to the new converts in response to the prayer of these two leaders. Amongst the believers was Simon Magus, a man who had formerly amazed the people with his teaching and sorceries, and who had secured a large following. He now offered money that he might have the power to confer the Holy Ghost upon whomsoever he might lay his hands. His request revealed that his heart was unchanged, and called forth a powerful rebuke from Peter coupled with an exhortation to repentance, an exhortation that was not obeyed. The complete story shews Christ's care for His own work, illustrates the double meaning behind the troubles that befall His people, and gives a solemn warning against an empty profession.

I.—CHRIST'S CARE FOR HIS OWN WORK.

To understand the events in Samaria it is necessary to bear in mind the instructions given to the disciples, and recorded in Acts i., 8 : " Ye shall be my witnesses both in Jerusalem, and in all Judaea and Samaria, and unto the uttermost part of the earth." That verse not only gives directions to the Apostles, but it contains the plan of the book of the Acts. The first seven chapters deal with the witness in Jerusalem ; the first part of the eighth chapter is occupied with the preaching in Samaria ; the last part of the eighth chapter, the whole of the ninth, tenth, and eleventh, detail the preparation of evangelists, apostles and the church for carrying the work further afield ; and the rest of the book deals with its spread to the larger areas.

Now, though the directions of Christ were so

explicit, the Apostles did not attempt to carry the work beyond Jerusalem. In the course of time they would doubtless have preached in Judaea and Galilee. They had no prejudices against taking the word to the rest of their countrymen. But it was not natural for them to think of evangelizing either Samaritans or Gentiles. A series of Divine interpositions were necessary to convince them that the Gospel must be carried to others, and that others were capable of receiving it and being transformed by it. So a persecution, originating in the hearts of wicked men, was divinely overruled to the scattering, instead of the suppression of the church. And wherever the members went they proclaimed the faith, and their proclamation issued in new converts. The first to be reached were the Samaritans, half heathen, half Jew. It was still true that the Jews had no dealings with the Samaritans, but in spite of that fact it was easier to have dealings with them than with the Gentiles. So the disciples were led out to the wider fields by the easiest route.

For "the uttermost parts of the earth" the initiative again was a Divine one. "The Spirit said unto Philip, Go near, and join thyself to this chariot." The Ethiopian eunuch, the first in the regions beyond to hear the gospel, had the good news preached to him through a direct act of God. Then the Lord Jesus Himself appeared to Saul of Tarsus on his way to Damascus ; and as a result

Saul was converted and appointed to be the Apostle to the Gentiles. Peter was converted to the idea of preaching to the Gentiles by a special vision, and confirmed in it by witnessing the outpouring of the Spirit upon the Gentiles. The church at Jerusalem was made willing to receive the new converts into fellowship by Peter's story of his vision and the gift of the Spirit in the house of Cornelius. The whole missionary enterprise was the work of the Lord Jesus.

The book of the Acts is now called "The Acts of the Apostles." When first written, however, and for about 200 years afterwards, it was simply called "The Acts." Whose acts were recorded was not stated in the title. It is true that the book contains the Acts of the Apostles; but it is equally true to say it contains the "Acts of the Lord Jesus."

Luke commences by saying that his former treatise "The Gospel," was written concerning all that Jesus began to do. The inference is that he is now going to continue the story of what Jesus did after He was taken up. A perusal of the book justifies this conclusion. The gift of the Spirit was His work. "He hath poured forth this." The formation of the Church was His work, "The Lord added together those that were saved." It was His name that made the lame man strong. The disciples prayed "that signs and wonders might be done through the name of Thy holy servant Jesus." The

Lord stood at the right hand of God to sustain the martyr Stephen in his last moments, and to receive him into glory. Jesus of Nazareth appeared to Saul on the way to Damascus ; and later, when Paul was in great danger, he said : " The Lord stood by me."

The Lord is out of sight but He continues to work. He is near to supervise. By directly interposing, thrusting out, and leading, where the Apostles took no lead, He showed that He was in earnest about the Gospel being preached to all. By this series of events He also interpreted the meaning of His commission to His slow-witted servants, and manifested His continued patience. At the same time that He was gently forcing them out, and by the logic of events opening their dull understanding, He was showing that He was particularly near to help carry out his own commands.

And this wonderful lesson remains. The book of the Acts is not closed. The book itself finishes in the midst of action. The campaign goes on, and the Great Captain still lives and directs. The orders " to the uttermost part of the earth " still remain ; and wherever disciples are willing to obey they will find Him near making obedience possible.

II.—THE DOUBLE MEANING BEHIND THE TROUBLES
WHICH BEFALL GOD'S PEOPLE.

The persecution was undoubtedly of the devil. But he has only limited power. He cannot do more than he obtains liberty to do. "Simon," said Jesus, "Satan hath obtained thee by asking." And Jesus also asked something for Peter : "I have prayed for thee that thy faith fail not." He did not pray that Satan might not have Peter. For disciplinary purposes, and for a knowledge of his own heart, it was necessary for Peter to find out his own weakness. The prayer of Christ was directed not to saving Peter from trouble, but to saving him in the trouble. Satan desired to cast Peter down and to make him despair. Jesus desired Peter to find out his weakness, and at the same time to have hope of recovery.

Satan got permission over the family, the property, and the health of Job, because he wanted to prove that Job's faith was due to sunshine, and that once he got into trouble doubt would fill his mind, and he would discard the God he professed to believe in. And God gave Satan the permission he wanted, because by so doing He could demonstrate the sincerity, reality, and purity of Job's faith. In the midst of all his troubles Job said : "Though He slay me, yet will I trust in Him."

Paul said : "There was given unto me a thorn in the flesh, the messenger of Satan to buffet me, lest I should be exalted above measure." His trouble was of the evil one. It was intended to harass and hamper him. And God permitted it because He had another purpose towards His servant. Such revelations as Paul was having were enough to turn his head ; and so a Divine, as well as a Satanic meaning appeared to Paul behind the thorn in the flesh.

Joseph said to his brethren concerning their action in selling him into Egypt : " But as for you, ye thought evil against me : but God meant it unto good, to bring to pass, as it is this day, to save much people alive."

There are troubles that are the works of enemies, of evil men, of the devil, of death itself, for death is an enemy ; and they are intended to harass us in the work of God, to wean us from it, to embitter us against Him, to reveal to the scoffing unbelieving world that faith is a matter of circumstances and sunshine, but that it withers in the storms, and cannot help us in times of trial ; and God gives liberty for all these to come to us because He can make all these things serve an opposite purpose. He can turn all the Devil's weapons against himself.

The battle ground of the great conflict is our heart. We can say whose purpose shall be fulfilled. By allowing troubles to sour us we can incline victory to the devil ; by allowing them to enlarge our sympathies, and to make us to cling to God for help, we can give the victory to God.

The spectators are the men and women of the world ; and, by the spirit we allow to rule us, we are furthering doubt or faith in other minds. But God is standing ready to aid us, and to enable us to be His witnesses in storm as well as calm.

III.—A WARNING AGAINST AN EMPTY PROFESSION.

Simon Magus believed, but his heart remained unchanged. He loved power still. Before he professed faith he gave out that he was some great one. People had great confidence in him. He wrought wonders to attach people to himself. His personal ambition remained after his professed conversion. When he saw that through the laying on of the Apostle's hands the Holy Ghost was given, he said : " give me also this power, that on whomsoever I lay my hands, he may receive the Holy Ghost." A faith that is only a change of creed is not a saving faith. Peter said : " Thy heart is not right before God."

Faith in God leads us to seek Him for a change of heart. The disposition must be altered. The prevailing passion for money, fame, or pleasure, is a selfish one. Sin is turning to our own way. The new life enables us to surrender our wills, to accept God's will, and to make the doing of it the dominant purpose of our life. If the prevailing passion is the same with us after profession as before, then there has been no real change affected, and our profession is an empty one.

Simon Magus brought his worldly ideas into the church with him. His faith was that every man had his price. He believed in the almighty dollar. Though a believer in the Lord Jesus he still thinks money the secret of power. He believes the Apostles can be bought ; and he offers money that the power of imparting the Spirit may be his too. Men measure other people with their own bushels. A man to whom money is everything thinks that all others put an equal value upon it. A man of the world ruled by money, and doing things only for money, cannot believe in the disinterested efforts of men like the Apostles. That money was to Simon Magus of equal power in the church, as in the world, was a proof that his heart was unchanged.

When rebuked by Peter and warned of his fate, if he did not repent, he said : " Pray ye for me to the Lord, that none of the things which ye have spoken come upon me." This again revealed the unchanged heart. He does not ask for a hatred of sin, or that he may be kept from evil, or that his heart may be made right, he simply asks that he may be saved from the consequences of sin. An unregenerate man will go as far as that. When a man is really changed he will keep from sin even though he see no evil consequences impending.

An alteration in religious ideas, a change of position from outside the church to inside the church, count for nothing if the heart remains as before. When the heart is changed God's will, and not our own, rules ; money takes a different place, we can then believe in men working for love, and we ourselves have that new motive power ; and we shall hate sin, and desire to be entirely freed from it, independently of the question of whether sin is visited by evil consequences. For such a change to be wrought we must look and pray to the Lord in whom we have professed to believe. Our faith in Him is to the end that we trust Him to do something, and yield ourselves to Him that His work may be accomplished.

XVI.

In Cæsarea.

ACTS x., xi., 1-18.

THIS is the first New Testament revival amongst
the Gentiles. It has been called the Pentecost
of the Gentiles. In dealing with the revival in
Samaria, we pointed out that, although the Apostles
were instructed by Christ to preach the gospel to
every creature, they took no steps of themselves to
preach to others than to Jews. God Himself had
to lead them out, and to overcome their prejudices
about the Gentiles. The old law was very definite
on the point of separateness from the nations; and
as that law was of God, nothing short of a clear
revelation of His purposes could make them feel
sure in treading a path that Jews had not hitherto
trodden. Therefore this revival was the Lord's work.

Cornelius, an Italian captain living at Cæsarea,
was a proselyte to the Jewish faith. He feared God,
and taught his household to do the same. He was
liberal in the distribution of alms, and much given
to prayer. One day, when engaged in this sacred
exercise, an angel appeared to him and told him that

his prayers and alms had come up for a memorial before God. It was God's will for him to know more about Himself and the way of life. If he would send to Joppa for Simon Peter he would tell him words whereby he might be saved, both he and all his house. Immediately Cornelius was obedient to the heavenly vision, and despatched three men to Peter to ask him to come and preach in his house.

While these men were on their journey Peter was being Divinely prepared for their visit. During a season of prayer this apostle fell into a trance, in the course of which God revealed to him that the old division made by the law between clean and unclean animals was done away with. Whilst wondering what the vision could mean the three men from Cæsarea knocked at the door, and the Spirit at the same time said to Peter that he was to go with them, and not to doubt but that he was being guided of God. Arriving with them at Cæsarea, Cornelius tells him his story, and how, and why, he had sent for him. Then Cornelius, having gathered a goodly company of relatives and friends, introduces Peter to the meeting and tells him that they are eager to know what word God has for them through him. Peter begins by saying how it was an unlawful thing for a Jew to have fellowship with the Gentiles, but that God had revealed to him that His purposes embraced all men, and that it was His will for all who sought Him to know Him. He then proceeded to tell the Gospel story ; and as he did so the Holy Ghost fell upon the company. The members of the congregation began to speak in the same marvellous manner as the 120 did who were gathered in the upper room at Jerusalem, on the day of Pentecost, when the Holy Spirit was first given. The gift of the Spirit was to Peter and his companions proof of God's acceptance of this Gentile gathering as a part of the Church of Christ. The ordinance by which believers were visibly received into the fold could not be withheld from these, and commandment was immediately given for them to be baptized.

Now whilst this work was of God, and was neither purposed nor organized by man, it was not done without human agency. There are three stories following one another in the book of Acts, at this point of transition from the restricted to the larger field of operations, which show the place assigned to men by God in the preaching of the Gospel.

An angel directs Philip to go the desert of Gaza. When there the Spirit bids him join himself to the chariot of the Ethiopian eunuch. The purpose of this heavenly guidance is soon apparent. The eunuch, like Cornelius, is living up to the light he has, and is diligently seeking for more ; and God answers his desires by sending him a man to help him. Neither an angel, nor the Spirit, teaches the eunuch the way of salvation. The work of declaring the Gospel has been committed to men, and the command has not been recalled.

The next story is the conversion of Saul of Tarsus. The Lord Jesus Himself appears to him on the way to Damascus, but in answer to the question, " Lord, what wilt Thou have me to do ?" directs him to a street in the city where it shall be told him what he shall do. Here Ananias, who is simply a disciple, being neither an apostle nor a deacon, is instructed to lead Saul into the light. He came to him that he might have his sins forgiven, and that he might also receive the gift of the Holy Ghost. The power of declaring how God forgives sins is not given to any particular set of men in the church, but to the whole body. In the conversion of the eunuch, Saul, and Cornelius, a deacon, a disciple, and an apostle, respectively tell them words whereby they may be saved.

In the case of Cornelius an angel appears to him ; but it is a man who has to preach to him the Gospel. There is no case on record in which the truth about God and salvation has come to men other than through human agency. In human agency we include the Bible, for that has been penned, translated, printed, and circulated by men. It is a tremendous privilege that God has conferred upon us in making us the channels of the knowledge of His will to our fellow-men. But the privilege is a great responsibility. It means that there are people in the world who will not know the truth if we do not take it or send it to them. Every one of us must take a share in the work, for it is committed to the whole body. Prejudice, however, is hindering, to-day as in the days of Peter, the Word from being taken to some. Members of the Church of Christ have failed to grasp the earnestness and meaning of Christ's command. But the providential leadings are as clear now as in Peter's case. After a century of missions it has been demonstrated that there is not a single nation or tribe upon the face of the earth incapable of receiving the Gospel and being improved by it. Wherever the story of Jesus and His love has been told there are to be found witnesses to the fact that God desires men of every kindred, tribe, and tongue to know Him, and to be blessed by Him.

We must also notice that though this work of taking the Gospel to the Gentiles was of God it was not accomplished without prayer.

Cornelius was a man of prayer. He was living up to the light that he had. But he was in the dark upon many matters. More light came to him as he prayed. Direction how to get more light was granted to him as he waited before God. God judges us according to the light we have. Behind this proposition many a man shelters himself who has no right to do so. Because their consciences do not trouble them upon certain matters, men make out that they are perfectly free to act as they are doing. There are things they have not seen to be wrong. They live up to the light they have. That may all be true, but the question remains, Are they seeking for more light ? Are they acknowledging that whilst they have some light, they also have much darkness ? Are they content with their little light ? Are they satisfied for any darkness to remain ? We shall be judged by the light we have, and by the light we might have had. Living according to our light includes using that light for the purpose of gaining more. Cornelius did not know God perfectly, but he knew sufficient to enable him to pray; and as he prayed he was put in the way of more light ; and the opportunity for getting more he eagerly seized.

In this event there was also prayer on Peter's side. Peter was a man of strong prejudices. His upbringing and surroundings accounted for them. They were so strong that some of them outlived a three years' companionship with Christ. The Resurrection, and the teaching of the forty days until the Ascension, did not dispel them all. Even Pentecost did not sweep all away. But Peter was a man of prayer ; and prayer gave God the opportunity He wanted to perfect the ideas of His servant. As Peter prayed, and as he obeyed, the strongest of his prejudices melted.

You may say that prejudice is a matter of upbringing, and that we cannot help our faith. We certainly cannot help starting in life with certain prejudices. The more and the stronger these are the greater will be the hindrance to our advance in spiritual things and to our usefulness. But we can help retaining them. Under the influence of regular, earnest, sincere prayer our ideas will be corrected, and our sympathies enlarged. We may have no vision as in the case of Peter, but we have the completed Word from which there is much light yet to break out, and which is still interpreted, as in Peter's day, by the course of events. The century of missions recently completed, is a modern providential commentary upon Christ's commands and God's purposes.

Prayer not only brings more light, and corrects prejudices, but it prepares us to hear God's call. If Peter had not prayed he would not have recognized a Divine call behind the invitation from Cornelius. The call to Peter was an outward and an inward one, of God and of man. The vision was of God. The Spirit said to him, " Behold three men seek thee. Arise, therefore, and get thee down, and go with them, doubting nothing ; for I have sent them." The inner and the outer voices blended. The events providentially coincided with the vision beheld, and the voice heard, only by Peter.

Some people say they have no call to work for God. That is not true. God has given to every man his work. But it is true that some people have not heard the call. The call is a still small voice, and it is heard only by the soul that has withdrawn from the world, and is waiting before God. Some of our ears are only open to the world's sounds, to its business, pleasure, excitement, and crimes. The daily newspaper conveys much more to us than God's Word. The voice of God is drowned.

Isaiah was one day in the Temple. He was waiting before God. Presently the vision of God filled him. Everything else retreated. The whole horizon was ablaze with Deity. Then he began to hear voices. He caught the sound of sacred song. The seraphim cried one unto another, " Holy, holy, holy is the Lord of Hosts ; the whole earth is full of His glory." The contrast was so great to that with which Isaiah was familiar that he said, " Woe is me ! for I am unclean ; because I am a man of unclean lips, and I dwell in the midst of an unclean people." But Isaiah waited on. His lips were cleansed. He was told his iniquity was taken away, and his sin purged. Still he waited, and then came the call. " I heard the voice of the Lord saying, Whom shall I send, and who will go for us ?" By long waiting Isaiah was prepared for this, and also for the response, " Here am I ; send me."

Jesus one day pointed out to His disciples the ripening harvest field, and He said : " Pray ye therefore the Lord of the harvest, that He will send forth labourers into His harvest." Then from the praying band He chose the twelve. Prayer about the field prepared them to hear the call.

All expansion of God's work calls for a direct putting forth of Divine power ; but the expansion means, on man's side, enlarged ideas and sympathies, readiness for enterprise, susceptibility to the leading of the Holy Spirit ; and for these qualifications, prayer is absolutely necessary.

XVII.

In Antioch.

"The disciples were called Christians first in
Antioch."—ACTS xi. 26.

OUR subject is the revival in Antioch. As our
text is suggestive of the principal features of
that event, I prefer to deal with it by explaining the
origin of the term Christian rather than by following
our usual course of telling the story first and then
afterwards dealing with the lessons.

I.—THE ORIGIN OF THE NAME CHRISTIAN IS A
TESTIMONY TO THE GROWTH OF THE FAITH.

The name was first applied to the disciples in a
Gentile capital. Antioch at the time was the third city
of the world. It was called the Queen of the East,
and had a population of about half a million.

The Jews in Jerusalem would not have applied
the title to the disciples there. All the Jews believed
in a Messiah, though only a few, proportionately,
accepted Jesus as the Christ. The majority would
never have called the disciples by a name which
implied that only a section of their race had a faith

about the Christ. The Jews called the disciples the Nazarenes. They had a proverb, " Can any good thing come out of Nazareth ? " and Nazarenes was intended as a term of reproach. Sometimes the disciples were called the " sect of the way."

In Antioch the name was not given while the disciples only included Jews. While the gospel was confined to Jews the disciples would only be a Jewish sect, and the Gentiles would have no need for a separate designation of them. The term Jew was comprehensive enough for all the various sects —Pharisees, Sadducees, Zealots, and Nazarenes. Their attitude to Jewish differences of creed is expressed in the words of Gallio : " If they are questions about words and names and your own law, look to it yourselves ; I am not minded to be a judge of these matters." But when Gentiles believed and were joined unto the disciples, a new term was required. The name Christian is testimony that the faith had grown, and that it now embraced Jews and Gentiles.

The work at Antioch, like that in Samaria, was the outcome of the persecution which arose upon the death of Stephen. The scattered disciples, who preached the gospel wherever they went, had come to Antioch. *En route* the message had been given only to Jews. But at Antioch some of the foreign-born Jews, men of Cyprus and Cyrene, ventured to speak to the Gentiles. The hand of the

Lord was with them ; a great number believed and turned unto the Lord. The report of this new development reached the church at Jerusalem. This body had already been prepared by the events at Cæsarea to welcome the Gentiles into fellowship, and so Barnabas was sent to look into the work. He was delighted with what he saw, and entered enthusiastically into the larger field of work, and much people were again added to the Lord. The work grew to such an extent that Barnabas sought out Saul, and after these two had laboured with great success for a year we get the record of the name Christian being applied to the disciples.

The word Christian is a cosmopolitan one. The idea of the Christ we owe to the Hebrew ; the word Christian itself is Grecian ; but the terminology of the word is Latin. Like the inscription on the Cross, which was written in Hebrew, Greek and Latin, the word is suggestive of the conquest destined for the faith over the whole world. There is many a true word spoken in jest ; and amongst the jokes of history which have proved true must be reckoned the words on the Cross and the description of the disciples at Antioch. The inscription on the Cross, " Jesus, the King of the Jews," was placed there in irony by Pilate as a bit of revenge for the threat to cite him before Cæsar. The Jews said, " Write not the King of the Jews ; but that he said, I am the King of the Jews." But Pilate answered,

"What I have written I have written." The term Christian was at first a nickname given to the disciples by their heathen enemies. But it was prophetic of the cosmopolitan character of the faith it described.

It was fitting it should originate in a Gentile city, where Jews and Gentiles were first united in a common faith, and in connection with the church which became the first missionary church in the world, for it was at Antioch that the missionary movement was born. The church of that city was the first to organize and send out missionaries, which it did when it sent forth Barnabas and Saul. The origin of the word Christian is testimony to the enlargement of the Church, and of its capacity for extension.

II.—THE NAME CHRISTIAN WAS AT FIRST ONE OF REPROACH.

We have already seen that it did not originate with the Jews. Neither did it originate with the disciples. They called themselves "disciples," "brethen," "believers." We have no evidence that they ever used this term in addressing one another. The Apostle Paul was present at the birth of the name. All his epistles were written years after it had been coined, and when it had gained considerable currency, but not one of these that have come down to us contain any reference to this description of the disciples. He wrote to those " called saints."

Apart from our text there are only two other places in the New Testament where the word Christian is used, and in each of these it is a term applied from the outside. As Paul grew earnest in his defence before Agrippa, that king observed that the apostle was doing something other than explaining his personal position. He was endeavouring to win his judge to Christ; and in astonishment the king cried out, " Thou wouldst fain make me ·a Christian." Peter, in his first epistle, deals with the reproaches that are levelled at his readers. He urges them to be careful not to suffer as murderers or thieves, but not to be ashamed if they are reproached as Christians. Jesus was crucified with thieves. He was classed with the criminal population. His followers were similarly pilloried. The term Christian was at first one of reproach, being used with the words thieves and murderers; and the disciples had to be exhorted to bear it patiently. They had to be taught that it was a name to glory in. Given to them by their enemies, it was years before they became reconciled to it and gloried in it. Eventually it became an honourable name, but at first it was a term of reproach.

III.—THE NAME CHRISTIAN IS SUGGESTIVE OF SOME OF THE CHARACTERISTICS OF THE FIRST DISCIPLES.

If this name was first applied to the disciples

by the heathen, what a testimony there is in it to their activity. This word becomes their monument. It tells us they were always talking about Christ. The thing that struck the outsider was the name of Christ. Not anxious inquirers, but scoffing heathen, caught this name and dubbed them Christians. Their zeal was not concerning a doctrinal or an ecclesiastical system, nor about ceremonies, but about a Person. The story of His Life, Death, and Resurrection was always upon their lips. They could not keep quiet about His Love.

And not only is this name a testimony to the principal topic of their conversation—it is witness to their evangelistic zeal. They did not speak of Him with bated breath behind closed doors. If they had only mentioned His name when they came together for worship, the world would never have caught at this as the outstanding thing in their lives. For the heathen to have called the disciples Christians is proof of how constantly they spoke of Christ to the world.

The origin of the word suggests to us the question, Why are we called Christians? Has our birth determined it? Is it because we have been born members of a nation that is designated Christian? or because we have been born into a Christian family? Is it because we are church-goers and members? Or is it because there is something about our spirit and speech and activity which identifies us with Christ? Do men regard us as being linked to a Christian body, or as being united to Jesus? Are His interests and ours identified?

It was the disciples who were called Christians. It was men who spoke to the Greeks, preaching the Lord Jesus. It was not the activity of leaders, but the work of the rank and file that called forth the name. The faith obtained its first hold in Antioch, and grew in that city, because those who believed were always talking about Jesus. We want the same kind of thing to-day; and when Christians talk about Him after whom they are called, the hand of the Lord will be with them, and much people will be added to the Lord. Many say they have not the gift of speech. The gift of public speech they may not have, but the power of conversational speech is denied to few people in possession of their senses. When people are interested in a subject they seek to know something about it, and it is not long before they can talk about it. The very people who complain of not having the gift of speech can talk volubly about shares, sports, politics, babies, servants, dress, and their neighbours. The lack of speech about Christ is due to lack of interest in Him. He is not the dominant thought in our minds. But if Christianity is to spread He must occupy the first place in heart and thought.

IV.—The name Christian was Made
Honourable by its Bearers.

It was redeemed from reproach by the spirit and lives and characters of the disciples. It has been frequently since a term of reproach as at the first. Once having been made honourable, it has generally become a term of reproach again when the bearers of it have been formal in the profession of their faith. It is committed to human care. It bears reproach or honour according to the lives of its bearers. The prayer taught us by Jesus concerning the Father, "Hallowed be Thy Name," is one we can well use about Christ. The character of Christ is unaffected by our prayers. We cannot add to or take from His infinite perfections. But His reputation is another matter. He will be ill-spoken of, or well-spoken of, according as we misrepresent or truly represent Him.

As the name Christian, as first used, is suggestive of growth, inclusion, and cosmopolitanness, we should seek to be wide in our sympathies, desiring the gospel of Christ to reach and embrace all for whom it is intended. If we have no interest in the missionary question the name is out of place with us. The name is not a sectarian one, neither is it a national one. It is wider than all these. It is truly Catholic. To be a Christian is to be one who loves all men, and who desires to see all men coming to Christ.

Those who gave the disciples the name of Christian had no intention of suggesting all that it does to us ; but we should not, on that account, be hindered from extracting all the sweetness that is possible from a name that was first given in bitterness. The disciples were not called Jesuits after Jesus, but Christians after Christ. Jesus was our Lord's name as a man—a name common amongst the Jews at the time. But Christ is His official title, the one that describes His office and work. Christ means Anointed. And the purpose of His anointing is described in the words, " The Spirit of the Lord is upon me, because He hath anointed me to preach good tidings to the poor : He hath sent me to proclaim release to the captives, and recovering of sight to the blind, to set at liberty them that are bruised, to proclaim the acceptable year of the Lord." This describes His mission. We who are named after the Anointed are also anointed ; and like Him we are sent into the world for a purpose. " As Thou hast sent Me into the world," said Christ to His Father, " even so have I sent them into the world." He came in His Father's name. We are sent forth in His name. As Christians we represent Christ, and are appointed to do His work.

XVIII.

In Europe.

ACTS xvi. 6-15.

IN dealing with the revivals recorded in the Acts,
we have omitted many important centres
wherein great spiritual blessings were experienced.
These articles would reach a much larger total if all
the New Testament revivals were included. We
have therefore contented ourselves with dealing with
those that can be characterized as turning points, or
beginnings of new things. As the Book of Genesis
is a book of beginnings, so the Book of Acts can be
similarly described. The gift of the Spirit meant
the beginning of a whole series of movements.
Pentecost was the commencement of the Christian
Church. But the church of Jerusalem was entirely
a Jewish one. The revival in Samaria was the beginning of the work outside the Jewish nation. The
work at Caesarea was the first to reach the Gentiles.
Antioch first included Jews and Gentiles in one local
church. It was at this latter place that the disciples
were first called Christians ; and it was from this city
that the first missionaries, Saul and Barnabas, were

sent on their first missionary tour. Before we have completed the series of beginnings, we must deal with the coming of the gospel to Europe.

The passage named at the head of this article deals with one of the turning points of history. The significance of the events which turned Paul's steps to Europe is more clearly seen to-day than at the time. By Divine leading the Apostle's course was blocked in Asia. At Troas he was on the edge of Asia, with Europe on the opposite shore. At this place he has a vision, in which a man of Macedonia stands on the other side of the water and beckons for aid. Coupled with the closed door in Asia, this is accepted as indicating an open one in Europe. And Paul, with Timothy and Silas, immediately starts for the new field.

As the course of Empire had moved westwards, so the centre of Christianity was destined to move in the same direction. If it had not done so, history to-day would be very different from what it is. The civilizations of Greece and Rome were great, but they were corrupt, and the process of decay had commenced. The infusion of Christianity arrested the decay, and in course of time started these civiliza- i ons on the upgrade. The civilization of to-day is inherited from that time. The best of the whole has been conserved by the salt of the Christian faith. If Christianity had not come to Europe, Europe would have sunk into barbarism and savagery.

On the other hand, if Christianity had gone eastwards through Persia, and India, China, and Japan, the civilizations of those parts would have felt the power of the new faith, and would have become progressive. The leadership of the world would have passed to them. America might have been discovered from the other side, and missionaries would have poured forth from the Eastern nations to the Western, instead of as now the West sending to the East.

It is well to note that the events that turned the course of human history were Divine. Great as was the evangelistic zeal of Paul, he did not propose the European tour. His heart was in Asia, and his efforts were towards the older continent. It was the Spirit that forbade him, and Paul eventually concluded from the course of events that God called him to Europe. There are events in human history that are Divinely appointed. What governs the Divine choice at these great crises we cannot fully say. We know sufficient, however, of the Divine character to be able to say that the election of God of an individual or a nation is not that others may be abandoned, but that they may be more effectively reached. God's elections are to service. He called the Jew not that the world might be left, but that the world might be reached with the message of Divine love, and blessed. And when the Jew refused to pass the message on he was temporarily set on one side.

The choice of God that the European nations should have the gospel in the greatest measure means a call to the leading nations of to-day to be the evangelists of the whole world. The gospel message has been entrusted to the richest nations of the earth. It is significant that the gold mines have been given to the Protestant nations—to the British Empire and to the United States. And our condemnation is that we spend less on the evangelization of the world than on any other great and world-wide project. If we do not realize the purpose of the Divine choice, and recognize that we have been called not to comfort but to service, we shall find ourselves put on one side as the Jews have been. If our churches do not become whole-heartedly missionary in character, their candlestick—*i.e.*, their power of holding forth the light—will be taken from them. We have been playing at missions instead of acting as those Divinely chosen to a great work.

It is interesting to think for a little while about the first service in Europe.

What day the Apostles landed we do not know. There was no deputation to greet them as there would be to-day. They had to look about for lodgings by themselves. A few days elapsed before the Sabbath came round, so it is clear they arrived early in the week. Whilst it was useless to look around for a Christian cause, it was not an unreasonable thing for them to endeavour to discover a Jewish place of worship. Their practice had always been to go to their own nationality first. But there was no synagogue in Philippi. Wherever ten wise men could be found in a city, the rule of the Jews allowed for the establishment of a synagogue. These ten were not in evidence in the Macedonian centre. Not only did the Apostles discover no synagogue during those first few days, but they observed no Jewish features amongst the crowds that thronged the streets, for when the Sabbath day came round they were not sure that there was even a place of prayer for a few. "On the Sabbath we went forth without the gate by a river side, where we supposed there was a place of prayer." They had not got beyond supposition when the Sabbath morning dawned.

In the absence of a synagogue there was frequently an enclosure, sometimes open to the sky, outside the city boundaries, where a few worshippers would assemble every Sabbath. For such a spot Paul and his companions looked. They found one, but it was occupied only by women. To this little gathering Paul spake. He sat down and talked to them. The first gospel sermon in Europe was conversational. It was not rhetorical. There was nothing about it to dazzle. It was an earnest talk for the purpose of winning a few to Christ, and not for the sake of gaining a reputation for the preacher. And the first convert in Europe was gained at this service. Lydia was a Jewish proselyte. She was not a European. Her home was at Thyatira, in Asia Minor. She was in business for herself in Philippi. When she heard Paul her heart was opened by the Lord to give heed to the things which were spoken.

The opening of Lydia's heart does not imply a deliberate passing of others by. She was ready for a work of grace to be done. Her heart was towards the Lord, open to Him, and ready for the admittance of more light. As a Gentile she had come in touch with the Jewish faith. God was more clearly revealed in Judaism than in any Pagan system. She had accepted the fullest light that had come her way. And this prepared her for more.

Here are some things worth noting and emulating. She was away from her native place, but she was worshipping. The faith that had come to her at Thyatira was not left behind with that city. The habit of worship acquired there was continued at Philippi. She was in a city without churches and ministers, but she was worshipping. She did not wait for a lead. She was not spiritually helpless. In material matters she had learned to look after herself. The spirit of self-help, so strong there, she applied to the needs of her soul. In South Africa we are familiar with persons who are keen on material things, and know how to look after themselves, but who are very ready to blame churches and ministers because they are spiritually poor.

They are helpless, or profess to be, in spiritual things, and want a good deal of nursing, and that after years of Christian profession. They allow some low fever to touch their souls and rob them of power.

Lydia was in business, and yet she found time for worship. It would be truer to say she made time, for she was in a city where the Sabbath was not observed. All the business houses were open on that day. For Lydia to close was to lose custom. But the welfare of her soul was dearer to her than the welfare of her body. We must be prepared to lose material wealth if we would be spiritually rich ; and when business seems to crowd out the times of devotion, the business must be definitely and purposely abandoned for a few hours in order that time may be taken for worship.

Eleazer, the servant of Abraham, tells how, being in the way, the Lord led him. That is the principle illustrated by Lydia's case. Worshippers are in the way. Those who make a habit of gathering to worship God put themselves in the way for God to deal with them. The experience of special missions bears this out. Whilst missions are organized for the purpose of reaching the outsiders, it is generally found that ninety per cent. of the converts have been regular church-goers.

The phrase, "She gave heed unto the things," contains a word used to describe a ship that has altered her course. The ship is out at sea, but suddenly changes her course and turns into port. The course of Lydia's life was altered at that first gospel service in Europe. So far as we know she had no bad habits to discard, but there were new activities to engage in, new virtues to practise, new motives to influence her. She was baptized. She accepted Jesus as her Lord. She brought her household with her to the new faith. Her servants in the home and the business were spoken to by her about Christ. Then the hospitality of her home was offered to the apostles ; and later on we find the church at Philippi meeting in her house. There is room for improvement in the best. When the gospel comes, even to those who are not degraded, it calls to a higher and a better life, and makes such a life possible.

When the gospel came to Europe it came to good and bad alike. It made a regular worshipper like Lydia a better woman ; it changed a non-church-going pagan like the brutal gaoler into a saint. All classes need Jesus. All are the better for receiving Him. At home we have respectable people living without God ; abroad there are some characters who have seen the gems of truth scattered amongst the errors of the great pagan systems, and are sincerely trying to apprehend them. At home and abroad these people are the exceptions. The majority everywhere without Christ are degraded. But good and bad alike require our message, and can be changed and improved by its reception.